Navigating the Dissertation Writing Process

Navigating the Dissertation Writing Process

Finding Your Path From First Drafts to Submission

Megan L. C. Krone, PhD

BLOOMSBURY ACADEMIC
NEW YORK • LONDON • OXFORD • NEW DELHI • SYDNEY

BLOOMSBURY ACADEMIC
Bloomsbury Publishing Inc, 1359 Broadway, New York, NY 10018, USA
Bloomsbury Publishing Plc, 50 Bedford Square, London, WC1B 3DP, UK
Bloomsbury Publishing Ireland, 29 Earlsfort Terrace, Dublin 2,
D02 AY28, Ireland

BLOOMSBURY, BLOOMSBURY ACADEMIC and the Diana logo are trademarks of Bloomsbury Publishing Plc

First published in the United States of America 2026

Cover design by Kathi Ha
Cover image (pen) © iStock.com/pxpalette

Library of Congress Cataloging-in-Publication Data is available

ISBN: HB: 979-8-216-39030-5
PB: 979-8-216-39031-2
ePDF: 979-8-216-39032-9
eBook: 979-8-216-39029-9

Typeset by Integra Software Services Pvt. Ltd.

For product safety related questions contact productsafety@bloomsbury.com.

To my parents, Jerry and Kathy Krone, for their relentless support in all my pursuits

Contents

Preface

This journey you've embarked on, it can be incredibly challenging. It can feel like a never-ending stream of writing, feedback, revisions, learning about additional requirements, more writing, more feedback, and more revisions, and then formatting—on top of pressures to work, teach, publish, network, and attend to all of life's other responsibilities.

But it *does* end.
What you're doing here, writing a dissertation, it's *hard*.
It's also temporary.

If you are feeling tired, overwhelmed, overworked, frustrated, confused, and so on, you're in good company. Most of us—maybe all of us—who have gone through this process have felt these emotions when writing a dissertation.

Those of us who have made it through, we stayed up late to write, got up early to write, wondered if we were good enough, wondered why some of our classmates made it look so easy, wondered if we should send our advisor a reminder, took too many breaks, ate/drank/slept too much, ate/drank/slept too little, craved human attention, just wanted to be alone—and then, we submitted, defended, and passed.

And you can too.
This is *hard* and *you can do it*.
I hope this book can help.

Acknowledgments

First, I am so incredibly lucky to have the parents I have. Jerry and Kathy Krone have been relentlessly supportive of me, even with all the tacking and jibing I've done in my career(s). Thank you so much for your support as I've pursued yet another unexpected goal: writing a book.

Thank you to my brother, Chris, for your technical advice, for always being up for a chat about horror films and *Jurassic Park*, and for chasing waterfalls with me.

Love to JJ, who often kept me company in her designated chair next to me when I was writing.

I am deeply grateful to the team who reviewed these chapters and gave me their feedback: Dr. Cris Bravo, Dr. Patsy Butler, Dr. Conor McLaughlin, Dr. Rita Soultanian, and Dr. Preeti Vidwans. I am humbled that several of you chose me to support your work and am incredibly grateful that you have supported mine.

I'm also incredibly grateful for the kind feedback I've gotten from clients over the years. While it is always my goal to be supportive and encouraging when working with doctoral students and candidates, who are working on one of the hardest things there is to do in the academic and professional worlds, I never expect to feel that support and encouragement in return—yet you've given me that. Whether you thanked me in person, by email, in your reviews, or in the acknowledgments of your dissertation, you are the reason I felt like I had enough inside me to write a book to provide support in a different form. Thank you.

I feel so thankful for the DePaul University Faculty Writing Community. I've always believed that writing in community is good for the individual writers and the group as a whole, but this is the first time I've truly experienced it outside of a writing classroom. Erin Herrmann, I want to extend a special thank you to you for organizing and keeping the group going, no matter how many or few of us showed up to each session. It is because of this community that I completed this book.

I've been lucky enough to have a second writing community through DePaul's Writing and Publishing program. Brittany Kass, Lee Hartley, and Tori Carl, I'm so thankful we ended up in horror writing together and that you've let me continue to write alongside you. I can't wait to read your books, all of which are going to be much more thrilling and amusing than this one. Much love to the Gremlins.

I'm thankful for my former doctoral cohortmates and classmates, who have continued to support me, as I support others going through the doctoral journey. In particular, I am grateful for Dr. Conor McLaughlin and Dr. Kai Mathews, who always make themselves available and also inspire me, as they kick ass in their own good work in this world.

Thank you to my relentlessly supportive friends Laura Lee, Melissa Jensen, Stephanie Souvenir, Cassie Branderhorst, Tiff Tafe, Clint Ruch, Dan Burns, Sabrina Wilson, Hilary Montgomery, and Nick Montgomery. During years I was working on this book, I had some big wins as well as some significant challenges, and you were there with me. I am so lucky to call you all friends.

I need to acknowledge Dr. Grace Bagunu, Debbie Deas, and Jessica Dickson for encouraging me to embrace the possibilities and to do hard things.

Thank you to all of my friends and family who have supported my work as a freelance academic editor. Whether you've hired me, referred me, shared my posts, or liked/followed my accounts, you've helped me sustain this life and career that I love.

Lastly, I wrote my acknowledgments for my doctoral dissertation hastily because I saved it until the end, was exhausted, and was ready to submit. Here are some folks (not already mentioned in the previous paragraphs), who deserve some love for supporting me in one of the most difficult things I'll ever do: Christopher, Zachary, Lee, Mox, Kyle, K Rob, Dino, John, Danny, Brian, Chanel, Nicole, Evelyn, Brian, Peggy, Joe, Teddy, Corey, Leah, Rachel, Amelia, Louisa, Morgan, Christian, Brian, Ryan, Steph, Afsaneh, Paula, Cheryl, Heather, Maria, Mariko, Corey, Annie, Tara, Peter, Leilah, Warren, Rod, Marianne, Maureen, Adan, Mark, Sarah, Jesus, Tierney, Ally, Jessie, Ashley, Neda, DeJuan, Andrew, Andrew, Julie, Jenn, Corey, Mark, Connor, Jenny, Anna, Trevor, Josh, Brandy, Juliana, Nico, Jake, Vanessa, Da Jung, Erin, Kari, John, Adam, Hutch, Thad, Tyler, Dave, Kyle, Kyle, Denny, Dave, Matt, Feven, Kimmie, David, Christina, Mark, Frankie, Stu, Ed, Edric, Camp M–East, San Diego State University Sport Clubs & Intramural Sports, University of Michigan Alumni Club of San Diego, and the Mission Bay Aquatic Center. You all supported me, and now I get to support others.

Thank you.

1 How to Use This Book

I've supported hundreds of doctoral students and candidates in writing and submitting their proposals and dissertations in programs all over the United States. This book is a compilation of what I've learned over the years of helping students get to the finish lines of their doctoral journeys.

This book is not meant to be read from front to back, as a dissertation is rarely written that way. This chapter and the table of contents can help you identify which section of the book might be most relevant for you right now, and each chapter and section will have an introductory paragraph to describe what is included in that chapter or section (just like your dissertation should have). Whenever content from a previous section is necessary to understand something, I'll mention that. That way, you can jump around between sections to find what you currently need for your writing process.

If you are still settling into your writing process or feeling frustrated with this type of writing, I recommend starting with the first four chapters. This current chapter gives suggestions on general workflow and how to find what you need in this book. "Motivation" offers ideas to stay motivated, inspired, and energized at any point in the process. "Planning and Organization" offers strategies for planning and organizing the writing elements of your project, so you can save yourself some frustration down the line. "Important and Unimportant Rules for Grammar, Syntax, and Punctuation" reviews technical aspects that can be confusing—or even controversial—with an emphasis on the *Publication Manual of the American Psychological Association* (APA; 7th ed.) guidelines, common academic writing expectations, and "rules" (most of which are really preferences). The remaining chapters are specific to common chapters and sections of a dissertation.

While I have edited a variety of texts, in many genres and styles, my expertise lies in academic work in the social sciences, particularly in education and organizational leadership, and in APA style. At the time of this writing, the APA had published its seventh edition of the *Publication Manual of the American Psychological Association* (*APA7*). Throughout this book, I note when a piece of guidance is tied specifically to APA formatting and share where in the *APA7* manual you can find that information.

Which Guidance to Follow

While *APA7* has almost 400 pages of rules and exceptions to those rules, every advisor, committee, program, institution, and field has their own expectations and processes. If your goal is to complete your program, my advice is to default to the preferences of whoever gets to decide if you move on to the next stage of the process. That might be because they deeply understand the expectations and requirements of your program or field, or they might just have a preference that is important to them. Sometimes, you'll be asked to cut or change things that may seem trivial or things that may be important to you. Only you can decide which of those battles are worth fighting—and some certainly are. Push back when you need to, but keep your end goal in mind: defending, graduating, and pursuing whatever it is you see in your dream future.

Note: I will use the term *advisor* to refer to the faculty member who is supervising your dissertation work, but your program may call this person your committee chair, major professor, supervisor, or another title.

Assumptions

I am writing with some assumptions about the expectations for dissertation formatting, and it is possible your program or your specific project will require something different. Most of the information I've included, however, is adaptable for different layouts.

Most dissertations in the social sciences are laid out in five chapters:

1. Introduction
2. Literature Review
3. Methodology
4. Findings / Results
5. Discussion

In the following chapters of this book, I describe what is generally included in those chapters/sections and some tips on organizing.

Other layouts include the following:

- Articles: When the dissertation is presented in a series of stand-alone articles, usually bookended by an introduction and a discussion/conclusion
- Executive: A concise document, often without chapters, focused on implications for practice

You can still use this book with alternative layouts. In those cases, focus on the sections in this book that apply directly and ignore the instructions on what to include in each chapter when your layout needs differ.

The Use of Generative Artificial Intelligence (Gen AI)

Generative AI tools (gen AI), such as ChatGPT and Copilot, are becoming more prevalent in all fields and professions, including academia. That said, I will not delve deeply into this topic in this book, and the only guidance I provide in this book on that topic is in this section. The following is my rationale for limiting guidance on the use of gen AI, so you can thoughtfully consider if and how you use them.

First, gen AI, as a technology, is still in its early stages and is constantly evolving. Even if I were to include recommendations on how to use it, they would quickly be out of date.

An even bigger reason I am limiting my discussion of AI is that many scholars, faculty, and program administrators consider the use of AI in academic work to be an academic integrity violation. While it may seem like your doctoral pursuits have the end goal of a singular product—the dissertation—the goal is actually the entire process of deeply exploring an academic topic; performing ethical, reliable, valid research; accurately describing the research; connecting your findings/results to previous work; and providing informed implications and recommendations. That process is arduous and time consuming, and it is what academics use to determine and welcome new scholars into their ranks. Gen AI tools generally help with the product, not the process, which is why many academics avoid or limit AI for research and academic writing, though some allow it for very specific uses and with proper citation (see the APA Style Blog for APA citation guidance; e.g., McAdoo, 2024).

Another reason to limit gen AI use is that these tools cannot (at least currently) write competently about original research. Put simply: it doesn't know what you did. No matter how much you tell it about your project, it can't know the details, such as how many participants you had, how long interviews lasted, or what steps you took to protect confidentiality. Because it doesn't know those details, it may make them up. Then, you need to carefully go through any generated material to identify and revise any AI-induced errors to ensure your document is accurate and consistent. Those errors can be a red flag for other scholars, indicating you either outsourced your work to an unreliable source or are not capable of academic research and writing at that level.

Related, gen AI tools are getting better at identifying real sources, though they do still sometimes make up or "hallucinate" sources; however, they may not identify the essential and foundational texts from your field and that surface in your in-depth literature review. Meaning, any scholar in your field of study, including your advisor, usually has such an in-depth understanding of the literature that they will know if the sources are tangential, inaccurate, or just made up. They're reading your literature review to see if you share their in-depth knowledge and will spot issues, which will make them suspicious that you do not yet have a comprehensive knowledge of the literature—or that you are using tools to outsource that understanding.

Lastly, unless you are using very specific, paid tools, anything you input into a gen AI tool now "belongs" to that AI tool. Feeding it the work of others (e.g., the literature) can be copyright infringement. If you feed it your own work, you are gifting the makers and users of the tool your intellectual property to use however they'd like. While I have found some use for AI tools in some areas of my life, I never feed my or others' writing, research, or original ideas into an AI tool to protect intellectual property.

If you want to use gen AI in your academic work, I recommend the following, in this order:

1. Check any course and program guidance on AI use
2. Check course academic integrity guidelines
3. Check program academic integrity guidelines
4. Ask the professor for the course and/or your advisor

If, after all of those steps, you're still unsure, my best advice is this: *don't use it*. You don't want to erase all of the hard work you've done to get to this point, just to be found in violation of AI use policies or academic integrity guidelines in an attempt to save time.

How to Decide Where to Start

Some programs require courses that walk students through each step in the dissertation process. Others assign large chunks at once (e.g., Chapters 1 through 3 for a proposal and then Chapters 4 and 5 after the research/project is complete), sometimes with immense support, sometimes little support, usually somewhere in between. Others ask for specific chapters to be reviewed, as they are completed. Sometimes there isn't much direction at all.

If your program has a prescribed order, go directly to the chapters in this book for support in writing those pieces. If your program doesn't have a prescribed order or wants you to do several chapters at once, I suggest the following:

1. **Start with the literature review** (i.e., Chapter 2). Everything you do for your dissertation should be based on previous research and study. You must first look at what others have done before doing your own academic research on a topic. This is important because (a) you want to be sure you are pursuing a project no one else has done

before, and (b) though you may have ample experience in a topic area, there are still things you don't know, and you need to dive deeply into the literature to be sure you have a comprehensive understanding. Try to stay humble and read the literature with the assumption that you have a lot to learn.

2. **Develop your research question(s)**, in conjunction with your advisor. The literature should inform your research questions, which will then determine your methodology. If you have subquestions or more than one research question, make sure they are all directly related and can be answered using the same methodology. Often, doctoral students come up with several questions they want to address—but those questions would require separate research projects. If you are still interested in the future, you can pursue the many aspects of your topic. For now, pick one that you can approach with one study and that you can complete within your preferred timeline.
3. **Choose your methodology.** Once you have a thorough understanding of the literature and have a research question, work with your advisor and methodologist (if you have one) to come up with your research design, methodological approach, target population, sampling strategies, and data collection and analysis procedures.
4. **Write your methodology chapter** (i.e., Chapter 3). You can write this chapter as you finalize decisions about your methodology. Keep in mind that for your research proposal, this chapter should be in future tense: describing what you *will* do. Once you're writing your final dissertation, it will need to be changed to past tense: describing what you *have done*.
5. **Write your introductory chapter** (i.e., Chapter 1). Many students try to start with Chapter 1, but without a background in the literature and decisions made about

your methodology, you won't have everything you need to write an effective introductory chapter. If I could, I would say write this chapter last of all the chapters, but it's often needed for your research proposal. The literature will provide everything you need to write about the background of your program, purpose of your study, and any other items you want to introduce before diving into the depths of the literature and methodology.

6. **Conduct your research.** I recommend taking detailed notes about each step of your data analysis and collection procedures, so you'll have them for reference when you write Chapter 4. Also consider anything surprising, especially if it directly supports or contradicts the literature, as you can include these pieces in Chapter 5.
7. **Update your methodology descriptions** (i.e., Chapters 1 and 3). Studies never go perfectly as planned, and there will be things you didn't know during the planning process (e.g., how many participants will respond to a survey). Once you've completed your study, update the methodology sections of Chapter 1 and all of Chapter 3 to include any changes, add exact numbers, and change the verb tense from future to past.
8. **Write your results/findings chapter** (i.e., Chapter 4). You can write pieces of this chapter as you complete sampling, data collection, and data analysis. Use your detailed notes from conducting your research and use the time when it feels like you're just waiting (e.g., for survey responses, for participants to choose an interview time) to make progress on this chapter.
9. **Write your discussion/conclusion chapter** (i.e., Chapter 5). When you get to this chapter, you've finally completed all the steps of a major research project and can finally present yourself as an expert who has valid opinions. I recommend saving this chapter for last

because you'll be tempted to give your opinions prior to reading the literature and honestly reviewing your findings/results. Once you have all the other pieces completed, you can finally give your opinions and share your ideas on the topic—though they should connect to the literature and your study.

10. **Add front and back matter.** Front matter includes your title page and then generally some combination of a copyright page, approval page, abstract, dedication, acknowledgments, table of contents, list of tables, list of figures, and list of abbreviations—depending on your institution's requirements and what makes sense for your manuscript. See "Final Formatting" for more guidance in writing these pieces. While you can certainly work on your abstract, dedication, and acknowledgments at any point, it's best to save the other front matter elements until last, as placements and page numbers are bound to shift as you write and revise.

    Back matter includes your references and appendices. I've described reference lists in detail in "References and Citations." Appendices only need to be included if they are (a) required (e.g., IRB approval), (b) are essential to understanding your methods (e.g., the text of a survey for data collection), or (c) are extremely long and would have broken up the text of the paper (e.g., a table, dataset, or interview transcripts). You can include other complementary information, though I recommend keeping your appendices to a minimum. Often, your complete dataset or interview transcripts aren't necessary to understand your study, and they add dozens of extra pages that require formatting.

11. **Complete final formatting.** Now that you've got a full draft, attend to the final formatting, such as ensuring tables and figures are placed properly, checking for

widowed or orphaned headings, and other visual aspects of the document.

Regardless of the order in which you write your chapters, frequently make time for the following items throughout your writing process. It will save you a lot of time at the end, when you'll be exhausted and likely up against deadlines.

- **Update your references/citations.** Tracking and formatting your citations and references can be tedious, and it's easier to do this throughout the process than to try to track down and format everything properly when you're also preparing for your defense or are up against your institution's submission deadline. I give some ideas on ways to organize this process in the "Planning and Organization" chapter and in the "References and Citations" chapter.
- **Format.** For common items that you are including in your writing, such as tables and figures, be sure to check your institutional guidelines and *APA7* guidelines to format items correctly as you go. Adding items with the correct formatting will save you a ton of time at the end of the process, when you'll want to focus on your defense and celebrating.
- **Write your acknowledgments.** I recommend working on your acknowledgments whenever you want to get some writing done but you just don't have the energy or focus to write about the literature or your research. Expressing gratitude is a great way to energize yourself and feel the support of others who have been with you through this journey. (See "Motivation" chapter for more ideas on how to keep going when you know you need to make progress but just can't seem to focus.)

Lastly, keep in mind that everyone's writing process is unique. Explore a lot of strategies, reflect on what works for you, and just keep going. As I mentioned in the preface, this work is *hard*, intellectually and emotionally, but it's also temporary. If you're having some difficulties with the writing process, I recommend going through the first three chapters. If you're ready to jump right in, pick the chapter that best fits what you want to work on next.

2 Motivation

Motivation is something that ebbs and flows throughout the dissertation process. You've made it this far, so you're determined to finish, but the process can be time-consuming, lonely, exhausting work. Use this chapter for those moments when you just can't read, write, code, or run tests anymore.

This chapter includes two types of motivation and strategies for time and energy management: (a) things that inspire and (b) things that energize. Consider which one you're low on and see if any of the following ideas can help you get back to it. I also offer some general strategies to manage your time and energy.

Inspiration

Once you've gotten to the point of writing your dissertation, you may be tired of reading and writing about the same subject over and over. Maybe that subject is a passion of yours, and maybe it's not. Either way, if you're studying it, it's likely important to some people out there, and connecting with the purpose of this work can go a long way in keeping you moving along. I offer three ways to find that "why": (a) popular media, (b) experts, and (c) professional organizations and conferences.

Popular Media

If you're studying a currently relevant topic, you can likely find some pieces of popular media on the subject. Shaking loose the academic perspective can remind us of the importance of our work. Even a work of fiction can serve as powerful inspiration because stories link us to the human experience related to our work.

Revisit things that moved you in the past, search out something that's been recommended to you, or find something totally new. Here are just a few things you could look for: movies, documentaries, books (all genres, fiction and nonfiction), podcasts, short stories, poetry, spoken word, magazines, newspapers, websites, blogs, social media accounts, TED talks—the possibilities are endless.

If you've identified a problem, chances are someone has created some content on it that can serve as inspiration. Let someone else's passion reconnect you to yours.

Experts

Whether you're considering a problem, possible solutions, or even methodologies, there are already experts in this area and related areas. They can inspire motivation or help you organize your thoughts.

Consider names you've come across multiple times in the literature or big names in professional organizations. See if you can identify some experts and then see what publicly available content they have. Search their home institution's website, for a personal site, or on social media (e.g., LinkedIn, YouTube, Instagram). See what they've written, filmed, and shared.

Some content may be behind a paywall, but sometimes an expert has built up a big enough presence online that you can get some great information and inspiration from them without buying their new book or paying for an article. You may find someone's work so valuable that you are willing to pay for it—but first, check in with a librarian, as they sometimes know tricks to secure sources for students or have a budget to purchase new materials requested by students.

Professional Organizations and Conferences

> **Note:** While professional organizations and conferences are excellent places to get inspired, I saved them for last because they can be cost prohibitive. If you find a conference or organization that fits your topic, check to see if they offer scholarships or discounts for students, members, presenters, volunteers, and institutional members (i.e., your college or university pays a fee that allows free or discounted access for anyone within that institution).
>
> If you don't see anything helpful listed on the website, reach out to the membership contact to see if there are any opportunities for financial support. Mention you're a doctoral student/candidate in the field and, if you'd like, you can offer to contribute in other ways, such as volunteering your time or skills. Just make sure the "compensation" for attending the conference is worth the labor you would be doing in return. Reach out early—several months before the event—as individuals are often selected well in advance for scholarships, committee work, and volunteer service.
>
> Lastly, check out local and regional associations and conferences, which can be great learning experiences. They can also connect you with people in your field and in your geographical area, while possible being more affordable than annual, national, and international events.

Whatever your topic, there are likely multiple professional organizations that support scholars and professionals in that field. Organizations have differing structures, offerings, and cultures, so do a little research before paying to join one. Ask colleagues or see if the organization offers local or regional events, which are less of an investment and can give you a feel for whether they are a good fit for your needs. With the social isolation restrictions during the pandemic, many organizations also started and continue to offer hybrid and online opportunities, which can be more convenient and affordable, though they offer fewer networking opportunities.

Professional conferences are a great place to get inspired, as you can surround yourself with scholars and professionals with similar interests. Attend sessions that interest you, and if you find a speaker particularly engaging or knowledgeable about your topic, stop by after their presentation to introduce yourself and ask if you could contact them about their work at a later date or connect with them on LinkedIn. Some presenters and scholars will be happy to chat about their topic, particularly if it means supporting an emerging scholar. Keep in mind that you're asking for their time, so when you're first making the connection, don't ask them to do "work" for you, such as reviewing your writing or consulting on methods.

> **Note:** Always bring business cards! You can get them printed pretty cheaply these days, and you can include a QR code to your website or for easy contact or use a digital business card.

If they're offered, roundtables are a great way to engage in informal discussion with others, to learn, and to build connections. Often, there is a facilitator who has some items to cover, but conversation usually flows with the interest of the attendees.

If you're planning on continuing your career in the field or a similar one, it's great to get into the habit of presenting at academic or professional conferences. If you're new to presenting at conferences, I suggest first finding small, local conferences, as the smallness lends itself to friendlier attendees. Ask your advisor or peers about the conference culture, as some conferences are known for critique and in-depth questioning, while others are more collaborative and supportive in nature. While you want to find a conference that fits your topic, finding the right environment for your goals and needs is also important.

Conference social events, official and unofficial, can be another great place to make connections in your field. These events often involve alcohol, so before you attend, decide your comfort level with drinking with colleagues or attending events where others are drinking. It can seem like it is necessary to partake in the after-hours environment, but more and more, organizations have realized that they need to offer social events that appeal to attendees who abstain or do not wish to drink in professional environments, so there are often substance-free events, too. While social events can be a great way to network, you should do so in a way that feels authentic to you.

Apart from conferences, many organizations have some free resources on their websites. They may have their own academic publications (e.g., academic journals), which you can browse for articles on your topic or use to get a feel for trends over the years. If your institution is a member, you may be able to access some paid resources, or you could check with your librarian to see if it's possible to purchase access to materials for institutional use.

Most professional organizations have multiple social media accounts, which can be a great way to stay on top of current happenings in the field. Some organizations will host "chats," where they'll pick a topic, post questions, and engage with accounts that reply.

> **Note:** If you choose to engage on social media, consider if you want to use an account with your real name or a screen

name and what else you use that account for. You may want to use your real name to boost your reputation in the field, or you may want to use a pseudonym to preserve your privacy. Consider your goals and your purpose for engaging. For some social media platforms, I have two accounts, one where I engage as "Megan Krone, PhD" and others where I'm less identifiable. My professional profile has engagement focused on professional and academic topics, keeping that "persona" narrow and easy to understand, while I'm free to use my other account for activism and gossip about the contestants on my favorite reality TV show.

Energy

"What advice do you have for someone just starting their doctoral program?"

I've been asked this question and have seen it posted on various social media sites. I think my answer is often unexpected.

I believe the most important thing to do when starting a doctoral program and especially when writing a dissertation is to reflect on the people, things, and places in your life that energize you. Writing a dissertation is incredibly demanding. It can be exhausting all on its own. If you try to do everything else on top of it—be the best family member, friend, professional, citizen, hobbyist, and so on—you risk completely burning out.

Try this reflection to make some hard decisions and draw some strong boundaries. I encourage you to write this down and revisit it when you're feeling overwhelmed.

1. **Describe the nonnegotiable aspects of your life.** Perhaps you care for dependents, are responsible for paying the bills in your household, or have a beloved pet who

needs daily walks. Include caring for your health: physical, mental, financial, and so on. This list should include what you need to do to ensure you and those dependent on you are cared for and your responsibilities are met.

2. **Describe what energizes you.** Reflect on the people, places, and activities that leave you feeling happier and healthier. For example, I know I need a lot of sleep and time alone to decompress, and I always feel more energized with time outdoors and when I connect with supportive friends. Think about the last few times you left somewhere and felt more excited, inspired, energized, and so on, than you had when you arrived, and describe who/what made you feel that way.
3. **Describe the aspects of your life that drain your energy.** Consider which tasks, activities, people, and spaces leave you feeling frustrated, sad, angry, or unhealthy. This list should contain things you truly dread or bring you down. For example, events with a lot of small talk really wear me down. I also struggle in competitive social situations. I love low-stakes, fun competition (board games, pub trivia, and recreational sports leagues), but I hate when every conversation with someone seems like a performance or competition. Think of things that have a net negative. For example, while I don't love doing the dishes, I'm much happier with my space when the task is done, so I wouldn't list doing the dishes as a net negative. This list should be solely things that soak up your energy and don't return it.

The next steps of this process can be hard but taking them can make completing coursework and the dissertation writing process much more doable.

4. **Take out your calendar and whatever your daily to-do list process is.**

5. **Schedule in the nonnegotiable things.** Add work, family responsibilities, and so forth. Make sure you consider time for commutes. Unexpected things will surely come along, but just worry about the things you know you will need to do daily, weekly, monthly, and so on. For example, I had three part-time jobs while in my doctoral program, so I blocked off time in my calendar to work because I had bills to pay. My to-do list included things like meal planning and caring for my cats.
6. **Look at that list of people, places, and things that energize you.** Block out time for those things in your schedule and on your to-do list. I carved out time for physical activity, self-connection practices, and frequent social events. These things took up only an hour or two daily, leaving the other 21–22 hours for responsibilities, school, work, and sleep—as long as I also completed the next step.
7. **Consider the people and things that drain you.** Limit these things or cut them out entirely. For example, for responsibilities you dread, can you negotiate with a partner, roommate, or family member or can you afford to hire a service to do it for you? For social situations, are there organizations, events, or connections that drain you that you could let go of? This can be a very challenging process. During my doctoral program, I really had to learn to say no. Living in San Diego, I always said no to beach days because while I love beach and water sports, I get restless sitting on the beach. That decision wasn't so hard. What was hard was letting go of friendships. I had some friends who really didn't understand the disruptive experience of being in a doctoral program, couldn't respect my boundaries, or were hurt when I declined a social invitation. Those decisions were hard, especially because I knew my limited social capacities were temporary.

8. **Protect your time fiercely.**
9. **Make sure your to-do list matches your priorities.**
10. **Draw boundaries and say no.**
11. **Revisit this process when needed.** You will likely have to make adjustments by academic term or season. Plan when you'll do this next, so you are sure you will take the time to reevaluate.

When I say protect that time fiercely, I mean it. Do not skip your weekly sports league, game night, Sunday dinner, date night, happy hour, or whatever that time and place is that gives you the energy to get through the rest of the week. Consider it as essential as eating and sleeping. Holding on tight to those energizing people, places, and activities will give you the energy you need to sit through long hours alone with a screen. When you're tempted to bail, remind yourself that you *need* these people and activities to be productive. When others try to convince you to skip them, resist with all your might.

I was lucky enough to do my doctoral degree in San Diego, so every Sunday morning, I'd head to the beach, play volleyball for a couple hours, grab a breakfast burrito (Humberto's, I miss you) on my way home, and then spend my afternoons in my office reading and writing, energized from my morning. Sunday evenings, I'd head to my friend Da Jung's house, where she projected *Game of Thrones* on a sheet hung from her garage. Tuesday evenings, I practiced yoga at my local studio with my favorite instructor Kevin. Thursdays were for kickball with my undergrad alma mater's alumni group. Saturdays in the fall were blocked off for college football. I regularly watched *New Girl* and *The Daily Show* with my roommate K Rob. I had wine nights with my classmates turned friends: Grace, Kai, and Mariko.

I sometimes got comments that people couldn't believe I had time to do all those fun things *and* work *and* write. The thing is, *if I hadn't been doing those things, I wouldn't have had* *the energy I needed to work and write*. Life would have been a monotonous routine of moving between my computer at work to my computer at home, staring at a screen, feeling guilty for not getting more done.*

> ***Note:** That's not totally true, as my main part-time job was in campus recreation, so I was often on the fields, interacting with students, and having a ton of fun. I still had plenty of screen time though.

I needed touchstones to bring me back to myself when I was stressed and anxious. These practices were particularly important while writing my dissertation, some of the most stressful and anxiety-ridden years of my life. There were some days when I had to twist my own arm to drive to the beach to play volleyball or to the hills for a short hike because my energy levels were low, yet keeping those things in my life regularly is what got me through long, lonely hours.

You will not have time for everything and everyone. You likely had to give some things up during your coursework, and you may have to give up more when writing your dissertation. I gave up a lot of the time I had once given to leisure reading, travel, and tagging along with other people's outings and their idea of fun activities.

The toughest part, for me, was recognizing when a friendship didn't energize me. In some cases, I recognized unhealthy environments and was able to phase them out quickly. With others, I liked the person, but when I was with them, my mind would wander to other things I ought to be doing. Those relationships were the toughest for me to cut out because I liked those friends, they hadn't done anything wrong, and I didn't want to hurt their feelings. With others, they wanted more from me than I could give. I did the best I could to let go of my sense of obligation, knowing my time and energy were limited.

Some people will not understand, which can be really hard. I remember the immense guilt I carried about saying no, especially when a friend would give me a version of "You never have time for me anymore." They were usually right. My time was taken up with other priorities. Many of those same people forgave me because when I finished, I worked to build those friendships back up. Some didn't. I had to let them go. It was hard.

Writing a dissertation is an intense process. You may have a lot of long, tough, lonely days. Yet. If you take some time to reflect and plan, with the understanding that building up energy will be as important as using it, it will likely be less painful—especially if you're sure that you've built in regular opportunities for joy and treat them as essential for your well-being and your writing.

Time and Energy Management Strategies

There are limitless ways to manage your time and energy when writing your dissertation, and they'll vary in usefulness based on the individual. I recommend asking around, trying some things out, and finding what works for you. Here are a few strategies that either worked well for me or that others have shared with me.

Know Yourself

You may have come across specific advice about when and where to write. Most frequently, I've often heard a version of "Every morning, first thing, go into your office and start writing, while your brain is fresh." Maybe that's exactly what you need. It also carries the assumption that you have an office and don't have dependents or other responsibilities that need your attention in the morning. Personally, I'm a sleepy monster in the morning, and my brain seems to actively resist thinking before 10 a.m. While you can try out others' advice, you're the only one who really knows what works for you.

In terms of spaces, most writers like quiet spots with few distractions. Consider the size of the space, distractions (including pets and housemates), lighting, sounds, and your comfort, such as your chair or standing desk. Perhaps you like to work in public spaces, away from the distractions of home or the office, or perhaps you prefer your personalized environment, where you can do chores during breaks or have easy access to cumbersome resources, such as sprawling mind maps (see the section on writing individual sections in "Planning and Organization"). Maybe you like to mix it up.

After a lot of trial and error, I learned I focus best in the afternoon and evening, especially when I can take it easy in the morning: have some tea, catch up on email, meditate, and prep for my day. After all that, I can focus for longer periods of time, using breaks intentionally to work out, have a meal, switch the laundry over, or take a walk. I work best alone at home, especially if I have a big, flat surface, where I can spread out, and natural light. I avoid music or ambient noise. I also prefer having multiple screens, an external keyboard, and an ergonomic mouse.

When you have an especially productive or especially difficult writing session, take note of your environment. Notice when and where writing is hardest and when it comes most easily. Plan your writing time (and other priorities) around what you learn about yourself.

Gratitude

One strategy that can take as much or as little of your time and effort as you'd like and pays off nearly every time is to express gratitude. While it may seem self-serving to express gratitude to make yourself feel better, I like to think of it as a win–win–

win. The subject of your gratitude can feel acknowledged and valued; you feel cared for and energized; and the Universe has a little more love and kindness moving about. There are so many ways to express gratitude, so try out a few and see which leave you feeling energized. Here are a few that have worked for me.

Acknowledgments

If you feel like you don't have time to step away from your writing but are feeling drained, try drafting or updating the acknowledgments section of your dissertation. In this section, you can express gratitude to anyone who has helped you through your journey. Take some time to write out thanks for your advisor, your committee, the faculty who have impacted you, your cohortmates or classmates, your family, your friends, or any community or person who has supported you in this process. Generally, the acknowledgments are no more than two pages, so this can just be a list, with a sentence or two for each person or group. Even without a ton of depth, writing about your support system can be simultaneously humbling and energizing.

Personal Communication

While you can wait until your acknowledgments to express gratitude for your support system, you could also thank them *right now*. Give someone a call, shoot them a text, or write them a letter. I like to keep a stack of cute postcards (not location or season specific), so I can send someone a brief note to let them know I'm thinking of them. Reaching out to someone who has supported you or someone you care about can connect you to what matters and give you a little boost.

Three Good Things

One practice that I'm not super consistent in using but can be very enlightening and energizing is the Three Good Things activity (Greater Good in Action, n.d.). I learned about this practice from the Greater Good Science Center at the University of California, Berkeley. The center provides a ton of free resources and practices to support well-being and living a meaningful life.

The idea is simple: Keep a running journal where you write down three good things that happened to you in the last 24 hours. If you can, do this practice daily. Then, every so often, look at your lists to identify patterns. The idea is to realize which things are going well and which things bring you a sense of joy or accomplishment. I've learned that cooking, physical activity, and my cat often make me happy. Fortunately, these are constants in my life, and with this practice, I've learned these small, daily things are sources of joy for me, and I can treasure them a bit more.

Meditation

There are many, many types of meditation and ways to practice it. While I now mostly use the Headspace (n.d.) app, when I was in school, a few friends and I (love to Maria and Ally) would meet regularly to practice lovingkindness meditation—which would certainly also fall under the previous strategy of gratitude. It was a chance for us to gather and send peace and love to each other, ourselves, our loved ones, our communities, and the world. Each time, we'd finish with slight smiles on our faces, feeling refreshed and ready for the rest of our days. If you're interested in starting a meditation practice, try out a few styles, and see what works for you. Most apps, websites, and meditation centers have some free content or a trial service. There are even walking meditation practices if you are worried about sitting still.

Apps

I resist downloading yet another app to my phone, but there are a few I've found that really help with my motivation. In addition to meditation (see previous subsection), Headspace (n.d.) has tools to track stress, depression, and anxiety as well as an amazing sleep section, full of sleep casts (long, winding, peaceful stories with no plot), music, and white noise options. Finch (Finch Care, n.d.) is a cute app, where you create a buddy, set goals, engage in challenges, check in with your feelings, and reflect on things that are going well. It then compiles that information and shares it with you as bite-sized bits of data, so you can recognize patterns and consider specific actions you can take to allow for more joy and to eliminate stress (as much as is possible). There is a social component too, so you can send your little buddy off with little positive messages to friends. I also like Long Walks (n.d.), which is a reflective tool that can also lead to meaningful conversations with friends. You complete very short journal entries each time you log in, with prompts for individual reflection or to start a conversation with a friend. Of course, the list of motivation, health, and wellness apps is extremely long and is growing every day. I hope you'll share some of your favorites with me by email or over social media.

Small Writing Goals

Many writers find success in setting short, daily writing goals. With this strategy, you set a time frame or word count to accomplish in one sitting. You may do more than that, but the goal is to make progress, even if what is written isn't used.

I generally use a version of the pomodoro technique (Pomodoro Technique, n.d.; Collins, 2020), which is a specific method that can be used in any form of work, and many writers find it useful. In this technique, you set a timer for 20–30 minutes and after each round of work, you give yourself a 2–3 minute break. After four sessions, you take a longer break. With the technique, each session should be recorded, though I never do that. There are pomodoro apps that can track the time and rounds for you. I don't quite follow pomodoro because (a) sometimes I'm on a roll and let myself keep going; and (b) sometimes, earlier in the day, I want shorter work sessions and longer breaks, while in the afternoon, when I tend to be the most focused, I will have longer work sessions. I do, however, find that setting a timer and focusing on a specific writing goal for that period of time to be very helpful. Usually, I end up with something workable, which can be used with revisions, or something came to me while writing that led me to a new draft that I will use.

Another strategy is to set a minimum word count. For example, every day, when he'd sit down to write, Stephen King (2000) forced himself to get down 2,000 words before he could do anything else. He said that daily practice forced him to create material. Not all of it was good, but sometimes, it was. Sometimes, it was really good—or at least the idea was good enough that he could revise it to become something really good.

Whatever your strategy, let go of the idea of a perfect first draft. Instead, develop your writing habit and eliminate that feeling of being intimidated by a blank page (or screen).

Summary

These are just a few ideas to help you sustain your energy during this difficult process. Try a few and see what works for you. I've also posted about this a few times on my Facebook and LinkedIn pages, and others have generously shared what worked for them. I hope you'll share what works for you, too!

3 Planning and Organization

There are so many ways to plan and organize. Try a lot of them and then decide what works best for you.

> **Note:** This chapter is about general writing-process planning and organization strategies. For strategies in writing specific chapters (e.g., the literature review), check out the relevant corresponding chapter in this book (e.g., "Writing Your Literature Review").

One of the most overwhelming parts about writing a dissertation is knowing there are so many pieces and deciding how to organize them into one, cohesive narrative—all in a single document. The goal is to tell a story, one that leads to the next chapter (or your future work). Tips on how to organize specific chapters (such as the literature review) can be found in the sections of applicable chapters within this volume. This chapter focuses on general strategies.

Create a Literature Database

Creating and organizing the literature you pull for your dissertation is an important step and can save you a lot of time and frustration at the end of the process. I recommend using software (e.g., Zotero, Mendeley, EndNote), so all your sources can be saved in one place, with notes, and sorted into folders.

In addition, I recommend creating some sort of system where you can easily identify patterns and outliers. For example, I used an Excel spreadsheet where each article was a row in the spreadsheet, and the columns included things like design (i.e., qualitative, quantitative, mixed methods), approach (e.g., phenomenological, regression analysis, narrative inquiry), year of publication, target population, sample size, major findings/results, and major recommendations. At first glance, it might be hard to see how a spreadsheet with that much text information can be useful, but it helped me identify patterns in the literature. With such a document, you can quickly see if most studies are qualitative, demonstrating the need for increased quantitative data on the topic. Perhaps there are similar recommendations in multiple studies—recommendations that could demonstrate the need for your study. Maybe there are a handful of outliers that contradict most of the studies, lending credence for more studies on that topic. You can also quickly locate an article if you can't remember the authors' names or the title of the piece, as you can search by methodology and findings/results.

I've seen students use hard copies in an elaborate file folder system or a document that is color coded to visually identify specific aspects of the articles. This system works for some people but requires a lot of paper. It isn't the most environmentally friendly approach and is more prone to human error, but some people do better with physical objects they can manipulate.

Try a few strategies early on, and then stick to one, so you can be sure all the articles you might need are easily locatable and accessible. It's even better if you can quickly identify patterns in methodologies, findings/results, implications, and recommendations, as that will help you create sections and subsections on topics and subtopics.

Create an Annotated Bibliography

Creating an annotated bibliography may feel like duplicate work if you're using reference organization software and have an article database, but I still recommend keeping one, if not for every article then at least for the major ones in your field and literature review. When creating an annotated bibliography, summarize the study and the information that is most relevant to your work. That way, you can glance back at your annotated bibliography to either pull additional information or you can use it to remember the content of the source and decide if it's worth a reread.

Annotated bibliographies are also useful for future work, when you might be writing about the same topic for articles, conference presentations, proposals, and so forth. You can keep the most relevant information in one place for quick reference.

Write Individual Sections

The amount of content that needs to be written for a dissertation can be intimidating and overwhelming. It can feel like you not only have to know what to write about, you have to know where to start, which means you also need to know the order in which you want to present the material. Yes, you can knock out an outline before starting, but unless that strategy really works for you, I recommend waiting to figure out the order of the material, as you can always cut and paste, moving things around once you have all the pieces.

Start by writing individual sections. Pick a subtopic, assign it a heading (using the headings feature in Microsoft Word), and write about that subtopic. You can even write these sections in separate documents, especially if you're someone who can't help but be concerned about putting things in order. Keep writing and revising until you're happy with that section. You can also work on multiple sections at once, but again, don't worry about the order yet; just complete the sections.

Once you have all (or most of) the sections written, organize them. To do this, look at the headings, which, if you have used Word's headings feature, you can view easily when you open the navigation window, or, if you have things in separate documents, you can look at the folder. You can also use the following three strategies: (a) creating a mind map, (b) using sticky notes, and (c) having a "for-later" folder.

Create a Mind Map

Mind maps provide visual cues and connections to find relationships and flow in our work. I pulled my strategy for creating mind maps from the book *How to Think Like Leonardo DaVinci* by Michael J. Gelb (2000), but there are many tools you can use to create mind maps, some digital and others just with a pen and paper.

When you work on your mind map, look for the words, concepts, populations, or other pieces that seem to have a lot of connections to or flowing through them. For example, when I created a mind map of my dissertation topic, I kept drawing stigma as a barrier between people experiencing mental illness and treatment. Then, I realized I was also creating a flow where other people contribute to or detract from stigma, so I found myself emphasizing social interactions and campus cultures associated with education about mental health, knowledge of treatment options, meaningful relationships, reducing stigma, and increasing help-seeking behaviors. The mind map helped me see how the topics flowed from one to the next.

It can be helpful to do this activity multiple times and to use different sizes of paper, sometimes including everything and sometimes forcing yourself to be concise. I had a large piece of newsprint taped to my office wall. There, I drew a mind map and would add to it, as things came up in my reading, research, or writing. Then, when I saw major patterns, I would take it down, put up a new piece of newsprint, and start a new mind map with a focus on those patterns. Having this visual reminder helped me remember all the swirling subtopics, and occasionally getting up to add a piece was extremely useful in my process.

Mind maps also helped me recognize subtopics that, while related, seemed tangential to this particular research project. I could not see a lot of flow to, from, and through those words, which indicated exploring those topics in depth could be saved for later.

Sticky Notes

I recommend using the sticky-note strategy after you've written many individual sections (as described previously in this chapter). Take the headings (or major points that arose in the literature or your findings/results) and write them each on a separate sticky note. Then, using a large space, like a table, a wall, or even the floor, arrange the notes, with the goal of telling the story. Look at the headings chronologically, as cause and effect, as problem and solutions, as the biggest picture to the most narrow (see "Writing Your Literature Review" for details on these strategies).

The use of sticky notes allows for tactile engagement and lessens the pressure of committing to an organizational flow.

You can keep moving things around until they look right. Then, you can look through and see if there are gaps or overlaps—or things that are just tangential and can be removed (or placed in a "for-later" folder, so you don't lose all that work).

For Later

Sometimes, you find a great article or write a meaningful section, but when you look at the big picture of your work, you can't quite figure out where it fits. Perhaps you went down a rabbit hole and wrote several paragraphs on a topic that now seems tangential to your focus. I see so many clients who want to hang on to these sections, and they spend a lot of time trying to figure out where to put them—but they just won't fit.

Cutting really good work can be heartbreaking, so rather than losing something that seems like it could be useful, put it in a "for-later" folder. That way, if you realize what you found or wrote actually is relevant, it's not lost. Even if the items in your for-later folder don't prove useful for your dissertation, that topic was of interest to you, and you can use those pieces in future work.

The vital thing that a for-later folder does is that it lets you make a quick decision. You don't have to question or debate whether the piece is or is not relevant, where it will go, or how you will transition to the topic. Just set it aside, in a designated place, and move on for now. It'll be there, safely saved, if you decide to include it.

Keep the End Goal in Mind

As you try different strategies to get and stay organized, keep your end goal in mind: completing your dissertation, defending, and graduating. It can be so tempting to dive into tangential topics, to do infinite revisions, or to try to perfect your document. Resist those temptations!

My professor, Dr. Zachary Green, introduced me to the phrase "good enough is good enough." He wasn't encouraging us to slack off. Dr. Green always challenged us to create excellent, meaningful work. I took this maxim to mean that it's the process—the learning of the craft of deep academic understanding, well-designed research, and thoughtful description and analysis—that mattered, not a flawless product.

For most doctoral students, the dissertation is the first time they're engaging in academic research, and rarely does our first attempt at anything result in perfection. There's a reason why the common aphorism "perfection is the enemy of progress" exists. Complete each piece to the best of your current abilities, within a reasonable timeline, with a focus on the expectations and guidelines that are required of you to pass to the next step in the process. Don't get lost in unimportant details or side quests. The general goal of completing a dissertation is to prove to the academic world that you can craft, complete, and write about research at an extremely high level. Focus on that goal.

Once you finish, you'll have the rest of your career to dive headfirst into rabbit holes and to widen your impact—now with those three weighty letters behind your name.

4 Important and Unimportant Rules for Grammar, Syntax, and Punctuation

Education about writing in English is usually full of rules about what not to do, even some rules about things to *never* do. The thing is, none of these rules are true 100% of the time. Unlike the French language (Académie Français, n.d.) and some other languages with governing bodies, there is no single authority on the English language. Instead, there are dozens of guides and handbooks on grammar and style. While some things are generally consistent throughout these materials (e.g., subjects and verbs should agree; "She has gumption" instead of "She have gumption"), there is also a lot of disagreement, most of which comes down to preference and consistency.

Note: Most accepted rules, when violated, are flagged in software applications, such as Microsoft Word, Google Docs, and Grammarly. You can often just click on the indicated word (such as one with a blue, squiggly underline), and the software will offer suggestions to fix it. As I describe in this chapter, some of these grammatical items are preferences, so you may see slight differences in what is flagged across grammar tools. If you use grammar tools, I recommend always following the suggestions within a single system. That way, you can be sure you're not applying a "rule" one way because of the suggestions of one software system (e.g., Google Docs) but applying a slightly different set of rules when you move it to another form (e.g., downloading it to Microsoft Word); this can lead to inconsistency.

In this chapter, I describe common conventions in spelling, grammar, syntax, and punctuation for academic writing in the social sciences. I also note which situations are guided by *APA7* and which are instead common conventions in this context. This chapter is not a comprehensive guide on this topic. It provides descriptions of common issues that often stem from not fully understanding the style and level of this kind of writing, rather than things that are actually "wrong."

Spelling

In *APA7* style, the default source for the spelling of any term is the Merriam-Webster (n.d.b) online dictionary. If you're feeling unsure, that's the first place to go.

APA7 almost always removes hyphens from prefixes (e.g., *nondiscrimination*, rather than *non-discrimination*). The exception is when removing the hyphen would cause double vowels or other confusion, such as in *meta-analysis*. Again, if you're unsure if a word should have a hyphen (e.g., *wellbeing* or *well-being*), check Merriam-Webster.

Similarly, most words are not capitalized in *APA7*, including theories (e.g., third space theory; Bhabha, 1994) and academic fields (e.g., education, leadership studies).

While Merriam-Webster (n.d.b) is supposed to be the guide to spelling for *APA7*, you can decide to make exceptions based on the literature, expectations of the field, or even your own strong beliefs. If you are using a spelling—including capitalization and hyphenation—other than that dictated by Merriam-Webster, you should note why, so your reader understands the spelling is an intentional choice. See the subsection on inclusive language later in this chapter for more information on making informed choices for spelling and capitalization for social identities.

Grammar, Syntax, and Punctuation

I grouped grammar, syntax, and punctuation together because, honestly, it's not important to know the difference to write a doctoral dissertation in the social sciences. Because I know a few readers will want to know the difference, here are the most relevant definitions of each from Merriam-Webster (our default dictionary in *APA7*):

> Grammar is "(a) the study of the classes of words, their inflections… and their functions and relations in the sentence [or] (b) a study of what is to be preferred and what avoided in inflection… and syntax."
>
> (Merriam-Webster, 2023a, para. 1)

> Syntax is "(a) the way in which linguistic elements (such as words) are put together to form constituents (such as phrases or clauses) [or] (b) the part of grammar dealing with this."
>
> (Merriam-Webster, 2023b, para. 1)

> Punctuation is "the act or practice of inserting standardized marks or signs in written matter to clarify the meaning and separate structural units."
>
> (Merriam-Webster, 2023c, para. 2)

Even the definitions overlap!

The following are "rules" that have been discussed and debated by grammarians, editors, teachers, and many other "experts" of the English language (e.g., Dreyer, 2019). My suggestions for these items are based on *APA7*, common practices in academic writing, and feedback I've seen faculty give students and doctoral candidates over the years. As with everything, you should default to the guidelines and preferences of your advisor, program, field, and the like.

Follow the Rule

There are some things that I consistently recommend and about which I have never gotten pushback from advisors, committee members, or reviewers. While many of these items are simply choices, there are some academics who believe they are hard-and-fast rules, and unless you are writing a dissertation on grammar, syntax, and punctuation, you might as well just stick to the "rule," avoiding critiques about your technical writing abilities.

Avoid Beginning Sentences with Conjunctions

In academic writing, it is very uncommon to start a sentence with a conjunction (e.g., *and, but, so, however*). Usually, you can remove the conjunction or combine that sentence with the previous ones. If neither option works, reword the sentence.

The exception to this rule is if you are presenting a direct participant quote as verbatim. In that case, use the exact language they used.

Avoid Ending a Sentence in a Preposition

Some consider the rule to avoid ending a sentence in a preposition to be an antiquated rule. Merriam-Webster (n.d.a) even has a post that describes it as permissible. The reason I say it's best to follow this rule is because so many academics follow it and will notice if you don't.

For example,

I included all the items that the interviewees had responses for.

could be reworded as

I included all the items for which the interviewees had responses.

Even when the rewording feels clunky, I avoid ending sentences with prepositions because so many writers and scholars have held to this rule for so long.

Avoid Rhetorical Questions

Rhetorical questions are questions asked without the opportunity for or ability of the reader to respond. They can make a text sound conversational, and the tone of a dissertation should be formal. In addition, rhetorical questions can make it seem like you are leading your reader to certain conclusions. A dissertation should instead present enough information that the reader draws the conclusions along with you.

If you're tempted to use a rhetorical question, first, write it. Then, consider what your purpose is in writing that question to figure out how to reword it. For example, I've seen something like this:

That raises the question: Why did the participants enter or stay in a profession when they did not seem passionate about the work?

Your reader cannot answer that question, and it communicates an assumption that people should be passionate about the work they do in their jobs. That could be reworded as follows:

*Many participants expressed a lack of passion for their work. In my interviews, I asked follow-up questions about their exigence for engaging and staying in the profession.**

*More on first- versus third-person language and passive voice later in this chapter.

Avoid Contractions

Contractions are commonly used and understood—which is why I'm using them in this book, which has an informal tone—but they should not be used in formal academic writing. When you notice a contraction, spell out the words.

As I mentioned previously, there is an exception when you are quoting participants verbatim. In that case, preserve their exact language.

Use the Appropriate Relative Pronoun

Relative pronouns—*who, whom, that, which*—can be tough if you haven't learned the difference between them and when to use each one.

Who and *whom* refer to people, and *that* and *which* refer to things. Refer to the following example:

> *The participants* who *completed the survey*

rather than

> *The participants* that *completed the survey*

Who is used for someone who is a direct object, while *whom* is used for someone who is an indirect object. The direct object completes an action, while an indirect object has something done to it—usually. For example,

> *The participant shared stories about people who had mentored them and about people whom they had mentored.*

If you're feeling unsure, substitute *he/she/they* or *him/her/them* for the word. If *he/she/they* works, you should use *who*. If *him/her/them* works, use *whom*. Consider the previous example:

The participant shared stories about people her had mentored and about people who had mentored she.

That doesn't work. Instead, it should be this:

The participant shared stories about people she had mentored and about people who had mentored her.

That's a quick way to check if the word should be *who* or *whom.*

When it follows a noun or phrase to be modified, *that* indicates essential information, and it should *not* be set off with a comma. When it follows a noun or phrase to be modified, *which* indicates nonessential information and should be set off with a comma. The way I like to think of it is if *that* or *which* were removed, would the sentence still have the same meaning? For example,

Because she loves pizza, we went to the restaurant that/which *has the best pizza in town.*

If you remove "that/which has the best pizza in town," you are left with this:

Because she loves pizza, we went to the restaurant.

The meaning for choosing that restaurant is lost. Therefore, it should be as follows:

Because she loves pizza, we went to the restaurant that *has the best pizza in town.*

Now, let's say the sentence reads as follows:

For dinner, we went to JJ's Diner, which *serves the best waffles.*

In this case, we could remove "which serves the best waffles," and the sentence still holds meaning. The phrase "which serves the best waffles" provides extra information.

Use Inclusive Language

As a general rule, the best language to use is the language people use to refer to themselves. Make sure the language you use *exactly* matches the language participants use, what is presented in a study, and so on. If that language is outdated, you can simply state that you are using another person's words, rather than using the language yourself.

There is an excellent chapter on bias-free language in *APA7* (see "Bias-Free Language Guidelines") that includes fantastic guidance and several resources for using inclusive language. Rather than trying to summarize all of that great information here, I'm going to just comment on items I often come across when reviewing dissertations.

Race. In *APA7*, when color is connected to race, it is capitalized: Black, Brown, White, and so on. That said, there are some scholars who purposefully defy that guidance. Some scholars capitalize Black and keep white lowercase, emphasizing and giving power to the shared Black experience, while de-emphasizing white hegemony, suggesting there is not a shared white experience, and removing indicators that uphold white supremacy (Meir, 2020). When making such decisions, it's helpful to just include a sentence or two explaining your choice:

> *In this dissertation, I will capitalize Black when referring to Black people and the Black experience and will keep white in lowercase when referring to white people because...*

If you're having trouble wording your explanation, find a source who has articulated your reasoning well (e.g., Meir, 2020).

Gender. Gender pronouns should be used with intention and accuracy in academic writing. Whether you include gender pronouns will depend on your context and whether you are writing about the literature, participants, another person, or a group of people. Again, you should use the language that people use to describe themselves. For accuracy and if possible, ask them. If that is not possible, do not assume and instead use gender-neutral language, such as the person's name or *they/them/theirs* pronouns.

> **Note:** *APA7* supports the use of the singular *they*. It is considered a "generic third-person singular pronoun in English" (APA, 2022, para. 1). When I come across individuals who still believe the singular *they* is not grammatically correct, I first try to point them to the *APA7* style guide, with a page number (e.g., APA, 2022, p. 140). That way, I'm not arguing grammar with them, I'm just following the style guidance. If they still insist, my decision depends on their role in approving the writing. If that person had a big role in moving my project forward, I'd probably switch to using only names when unsure of pronouns because it's important to me to be as accurate as possible when writing about elements of identity.

When writing about authors of the literature, I recommend removing gender pronouns. First, you should always use the language that people use to describe themselves, and unless the author has discussed their gender and pronouns, you likely don't know for sure. Rather than using the wrong ones, use *they/them/theirs* or just use the author's name. Second, gender bias is still alive in academia (Formanowicz et al., 2023; Knobloch-Westerwick et al., 2013; Llorens et al., 2021; Teich et al., 2022) and removing indicators of genders when discussing researchers removes the (usually subconscious) temptation to assess credibility based on gender. I also avoid first names, unless I'm discussing someone who is extremely well known or someone who created a foundational theory upon which I'm relying.

Other writers and editors disagree with me and feel that gender indicators should be included to (a) increase awareness of gender imbalances and inequities and (b) broaden awareness of contributions made by women, trans+, and nonbinary people (e.g., Llorens et al., 2021; Sharpe, 2024). I understand that perspective, yet I find advocates of this approach often rely on assumptions (e.g., that first names convey someone's gender), rather than authors' stated identities. To avoid misgendering authors and to reduce bias, I avoid gendered language, including pronouns, unless it is known and relevant to the writing context.

Another common issue I see is the use of the term *preferred pronouns*. Saying someone's pronouns are "preferred" implies that they aren't accurate. Instead of that term, use *identified pronouns*, *self-identified pronouns*, or (my preference) just *pronouns*.

When writing about gender, *APA7* recommends avoiding the following terms:

- *Male/female*. These are terms that describe biological sex, and unless biology is relevant to your paper, these terms should not be used. Instead, use terms that describe gender: *woman, man, transgender person, cisgender person, genderqueer person*, and so on. In addition, male/female should only be used as adjectives, not nouns. For example, avoid "Females made up 40% of the sample." Ideally, you'd be using self-selected language that refers to gender (e.g., woman, nonbinary) instead, but if a study uses male/female language, the wording should be "Female participants made up 40% of the sample."
- *Birth sex* or *natal sex*. Use *assigned sex* or *sex assigned at birth*.
- *Man* or *mankind* (in reference to humanity as a whole). Instead, use *people*, *individuals*, or *humankind*.
- Terms that imply gender binaries (e.g., *opposite sex*).
- Disparaging terms (e.g., *transvestite*). Note that some terms that were considered disparaging in the past, such

as *queer*, have been reclaimed. If you are unsure, again, ask the person, defer to the language they use for themselves, or default to neutral options.

- Gendered endings: Use *police officer* instead of *policeman* and *homemaker* instead of *housewife*.
- *Transgendered*: *Transgender* is an adjective already, so use *transgender person, trans person, transgender man, transgender woman, transwoman, transman*, and so on.

Avoid Using Second-Person Voice

Second-person voice (i.e., you, your) implies you are speaking to the reader directly—as I am doing in this book. It carries assumptions that you know the reader's intentions or are giving the reader direction. That's completely fine in an instructional book. For example, I can assume that in picking up a book like this, the reader is looking for direct support and advice in writing their dissertation. It is not appropriate for academic writing, when you don't know who your reader might be, don't know what their level of knowledge is, and certainly don't want to instruct them to do anything. I see this happen most often when someone is describing something related to their study

> *When you look at the documents, you can see...*

or describing the literature

> *Researchers found when you experience discrimination in the workplace, you feel less psychologically safe at work.*

To reword the previous examples, I might use the following:

> *During the document review, I found...*

and

> *Researchers found participants who experienced discrimination in the workplace felt less psychologically safe at work.*

or

> *Researchers found workplace discrimination was connected with lower levels of psychological safety.*

The acknowledgments section is an exception to this, as you are actually directly addressing individuals to thank them for their support.

Avoid Using First-Person Plural Voice

First-person plural voice (i.e., we, our) implies there is more than one author. That might be true for journal articles with multiple authors; however, a dissertation is, by definition, written by only one person, so you should use "I" or in the third person (see following section: "It Depends").

Of course, your program may have allowed or required you to work with a research team. If that is the case, prior to using first-person plural voice, describe your research team and what role you had. Use *we/our* when you did things as a team, and *I/third person* when you did things as an individual.

> **Note:** In this chapter, I made up some citations to use as examples. To indicate which ones are made up and which ones are real citations, I've used the year 2050 for all made-up citations.

Be Precise When Quoting the Literature and Participants

When quoting the literature, you should use verbatim wording and matching punctuation. The exceptions are that you can change the capitalization of the first word if it starts a sentence and change the ending punctuation to match how the quoted material fits within your writing (see Section 8.29 of *APA7*). If you believe the meaning is unclear, you can add a word or phrase in brackets to add clarification. For example,

They indicated there was a great deal of uncertainty prior to the experience.

(Souvenir, 2050, p. 627)

could become

[The participants] indicated there was a great deal of uncertainty prior to the experience.

(Souvenir, 2050, p. 627)

When quoting participants, decide if you are going to quote them verbatim or not. Unless you are doing a linguistic study, it's unlikely you need to quote participants verbatim, and you can remove filler words and do not need to attempt to match spelling to accents or pronunciations. For example, "Like, um, I was gonna, um—See, well, I was gonna go, but then, well, I didn't" is tough to read. If you are not quoting participants verbatim, you could instead quote, "Well, I was gonna go, but then, I didn't."

It maintains the meaning but is much easier for your reader to follow. This is a judgment call, and your removal of filler words should not change the quote in any significant way. Even in this case, I did not change "gonna" to "going to" because it was more accurate to the participant quote and didn't affect the reader's ability to understand the quote.

In quoting participants, disregard other "rules," such as not starting a sentence with a conjunction or ending a sentence with a preposition. Spoken language is much different from written, academic language. Your participant quotes should reflect their spoken language.

It Depends

There are a lot of "rules" that really depend on the expectations of the reader, the context, and the writer's preferences. Here are some common things I see in dissertation writing that depend on the situation.

Avoid Passive Voice

I am a big fan of this guidance, as it's easier to read text written in active voice, and things can be unclear in passive voice. For example,

> *It was found in the literature that writing in community can be beneficial for individuals working on writing goals.*
>
> *(Kass & Hartley, 2050)*

is not as strong of a sentence as

> *Kass and Hartley (2050) found writing in community is beneficial for individuals working on writing goals.*

I say that "it depends" because some scholars still insist on avoiding the first person in academic writing (see next subsection).

Use First-Person Narration

APA7 recommends the use of first person, and I fully agree with this recommendation; however, some fields and individual scholars believe first person should not be used in academic writing. To decide what you'd like to do, check with your advisor to see if they have a preference. (They usually do.) If they don't, stick with first person, as it can be useful in crafting clear, concise sentences. For example,

> *During interviews, I used memos to bracket my biases*

is much more direct than

> *Memos were used during interviews to bracket possible biases*

as there is acknowledgment that there is a human researcher (which is exactly what some scholars dislike). I also just find writing about oneself in third person to be unnecessary and sometimes clunky:

During interviews, the researcher used memos to bracket their biases.

Again, this is a preference.

Avoid Anthropomorphism

Anthropomorphism is when a nonhuman subject is assigned a human action. For example,

The study considered whether...

Studies are not humans, so they cannot consider—and, as mentioned above, it's okay to use first person for clarity and accuracy (says *APA7* and me):

In this study, I considered whether...

I say "it depends" because, as mentioned in the previous subsection, some fields and scholars still direct writers to avoid first person. Some think that removing the human doing the actions makes the study more objective and, thus, more scientific. If your advisor feels strongly about using first versus third person, they'll likely indicate that to you in early drafts.

I still recommend avoiding truly human actions, such as considering, deciding, determining, concluding, and so on. There are some gray areas where *APA7* (2020) says the following are acceptable: *the study found, this section focuses on*, and so on (see section 4.11). I have, however, come across some dissertation reviewers who require even those to be rephrased.

Avoid Idioms, Similes, and Metaphors

While idioms, similes, and metaphors can lead to some beautifully written passages, it's best to avoid them in academic writing. Academic writing should be precise and clear, and idioms, similes, and metaphors can be interpreted differently by different people, especially if they have different meanings across geographical locations or cultures.

Summary

While there are accepted conventions in academic writing, many technical aspects come down to preference. As I've stated multiple times in this book, I recommend defaulting to the guidelines and preferences of your advisor and program, as they are the experts of the expectations in your field and decide whether your writing is at the level it needs to be to move to the next step. Otherwise, rely on *APA7* guidance and general conventions I described in this chapter.

5 Writing the Introduction

Note: I strongly recommend writing this section after you have written your literature review and methodology, as the sections in your introduction will be informed by the literature, and you'll need to have already made your methodology decisions for others.

In the five-chapter dissertation layout, the first chapter is usually the introduction, which generally includes a description of the problem, rationale for the study, and a brief summary of the methodology. This chapter is the hardest chapter for me to write about because expectations, requirements, and organization for this chapter differ greatly from institution to institution and project to project. Because I can't provide hard-and-fast guidance for this chapter, I'm going to describe items commonly included in this chapter, the depth commonly required for those items, and when and how to check to see if your institution's expectations are in line with those items. As with any part of the dissertation, before you start, see if your institution has a dissertation template, as that is the best guide for what to include in this chapter.

In the following, I describe the sections I see most commonly in Chapter 1, in the order I most commonly see them. When writing the sections, I recommend starting with whatever section makes the most sense, rather than writing the sections in order. Sometimes, in articulating one section, another section that seemed a little unfocused can come into view.

The Introduction to the Introduction

The first few paragraphs of your dissertation should serve as an argument about a compelling, urgent issue and insinuate that your project will provide vital information in crafting solutions to the problem—not directly solving the problem but providing much-needed context, understanding, or ideas. The tricky part of the introduction is deciding exactly how much information to include, how much to assume the reader already knows, and how to organize your ideas in a way that will compel your reader to keep reading to learn more about your work.

For most projects, I recommend a brief activity to figure out exactly where you'd like to start your narrative. If you're struggling with your opening, try this quick writing exercise, answering these questions:

1. Describe your study in the narrowest terms possible. Who did you study? Why?
2. What do/will your results/findings show?
3. What narrow problem will your study inform?
4. What other problems trickle up from this narrow problem?
5. What problem are you *really* trying to solve?
6. Then, take a look at what you've come up with and decide which of these problems seems the most urgent or compelling. That's where you should start your introduction.

As an example, I'll go through this activity (briefly) with my dissertation topic (see Krone, 2016).

1. I studied correlations between higher education professionals' levels of stigma of mental illness and knowledge of, referrals to, and engagement in on-campus mental health practices.

2. This topic is important to understand because student affairs professionals often have meaningful, lasting connections with students and can strongly influence campus climate, including the stigma of mental illness.

    a. There is a negative correlational relationship between stigma and help-seeking behaviors, so understanding levels of stigma can be used as an indicator of help-seeking behaviors: The higher the stigma, the less likely students will be to seek help. (Note: This is a correlational relationship, so stigma is being used as a [negative] stand-in for help-seeking behaviors, which are much harder to study. That, of course, was a limitation of the study, as this is not necessarily a causal relationship.)

    b. Most institutions have mental health services available, but they require help-seeking behaviors.

    c. Most students experiencing symptoms of mental illness do not seek help.

    d. Students with untreated mental illness are more likely than their peers to discontinue their studies, have strained relationships with others, and harm themselves.

    e. More than half of students on college campuses report symptoms of mental illness, even if they have not been diagnosed.

    f. Students are at risk, and institutions that do not actively connect students to help will have students drop out, strain relationships in the campus community, and harm themselves.

When I stepped back, I realized the most compelling piece, in my view, is simply the prevalence of mental illness in college student populations. While the conclusions from my results were related to educating and connecting on-campus staff, it was more compelling to start with a statement that more than half of students on college campuses report symptoms of mental illness and then the large percentages who have been diagnosed, particularly with depression and anxiety. So, that's where I started my introduction.

Once you have your starting point, make it compelling and, if you can, urgent. Then, in the next paragraph, describe what will follow in the entirety of the paper. Explain which chapters include which information (in a matching order) and include any general statements about the scope of the study, with a very brief mention of the methodology (maybe one to three sentences).

This style of introduction may seem dry and unnecessary, but it's important in academic writing, especially in a dissertation, to avoid any surprises for the reader. They should always know what's coming next. The reason to do this in dissertations is to demonstrate to the reader that you've thought everything through and have made purposeful decisions about what to include and exclude, all based on the literature and, eventually, the findings/results of your study. You want to prevent your reader from thinking, "I wonder if they considered [X] or did [Y], though." You just tell them you did.

Keep in mind that Chapters 1, 2, 3, and 4 of the dissertation are generally descriptive, void of your opinion. Once you've introduced the problem and study, described the literature, described your methodology, and presented your findings/results, then you have demonstrated you've done a thorough investigation, and you can add in a bit of your voice and opinions (as in Chapter 5 of your dissertation: Discussion).

Background of the Problem

It's common to present the background in one of the following ways: (a) chronological, (b) large to small, or (c) cause and effect. Your choice of these or other types of organization should depend on your topic. You present the background of the problem you are studying, tell a story, and whenever possible, make the issue compelling and urgent. Explain that action is needed to right the course and that any action needs to be evidence based—hence, the need for studies, such as yours.

Chronological Presentation

Sometimes the best way to present a problem is chronologically. This strategy works best when a problem started at one point in time and grew or became more complex over time.

For example, when exploring why institutions of higher education can't seem to attract and maintain the diversity of faculty, staff, or students they purport to desire, a researcher might want to describe how and why universities in the United States were founded. Then, the writer could talk about social movements that pushed for changes in access to education. They could give a historical account of policies, such as Title IX (U.S. Department of Education, n.d.) and the Americans With Disabilities Act (n.d.), to demonstrate how outside forces required institutions to change their structures to become more inclusive. They'd eventually move to current conditions and what influences them.

Big-to-Small Presentation

Another way to present the background of a problem is to go from a really big picture to a narrow topic. In choosing this organizational strategy, you're leaning on a big problem to make the study compelling and time sensitive. You're then narrowing in on the specific piece that you studied, demonstrating how it could affect the overarching issue.

For example, a researcher might present demographic information on incarceration rates, then on recidivism rates, and then keep narrowing the problem until they've reached the topic of structures that can support formerly incarcerated people in building sustainable living and financial situations, preventing recidivism and encouraging people to thrive—which then allows them to positively influence their families and communities, which could also prevent others from becoming incarcerated—with attention to structures that encourage arrests in certain communities based on assumptions of criminal behavior.

Cause-and-Effect Presentation

Lastly, researchers often present the background of problems as a cause and effect. For example, when exploring educational equity, a writer might talk about how income taxes are used to fund local schools, which inevitably leads to better schools in wealthy districts, where students already have increased access to resources, and under-resourced schools in poor districts, where parents do not have the funds to pay for outside opportunities. They might then go into further effects, such as how the differences in resources affect teacher recruitment and retention and other significant influences on the quality of education in an area.

Statement of the Problem

It may seem like the "Statement of the Problem" and the "Background of the Problem" would be repetitive sections. Instead, the background is how the issue came to be: what caused it or made it more complex. In the statement of the problem, you should talk about the problem itself, who it affects and how, and how practitioners and researchers have approached it.

Purpose of the Study

The purpose of the study builds on the background of the problem and statement of the problem. In those prior sections, you have described a problem, how it came to be, and demonstrated that it is compelling and needs to be addressed urgently. Now, you'll explain how your study is going to provide key information that can be used to prevent, delay, solve, or further understand the problem.

Explain what aspect of the problem you studied (or will study, if this is your proposal). Explain who you included as participants and why they were the right target population to attain the information needed. Explain how your methods led to the needed data and how your analysis teased out the information needed. Connect your study to the previous sections. Keep in mind that you are conducting research with curiosity—removing, as much as possible, your bias and assumptions—and your end result will be information that others can use in practice or for future research. You are not solving the problem yourself (with this project) but providing vital information for others to solve it or for you to solve it once you've completed this project and move on from your doctoral studies.

Research Questions

Your research question(s) should be derived from the literature and created with input from your advisor (and your methodologist, if you have one). When you write this section, you can usually keep it brief, noting, "The research question for this study is…" or, if you have multiple research questions, you can use bullet points to list each question.

> **Note:** If you have multiple research questions, be sure they are distinct yet can be answered with the same dataset and methodology. Remember, you're not studying everything and solving all problems with this one research project. You are focusing on a very narrow topic and collecting detailed, focused information. If you have a lot of questions about this problem, write them all down and then choose which one you want to explore *now*—or which one your advisor wants you to explore now. Then, save the rest for when you've got those extra letters behind your name and, hopefully, are getting paid well to keep doing this work.

Significance of the Study

In this section, you should describe why your study is uniquely suited to inform the problem you have described. Perhaps you're using a methodology that has never been used to study this topic or you have special access to your target population. When writing this section, consider the previous literature and how your study differs or builds on that literature, yielding new, valuable information. Once the study is complete, you can also briefly mention the implications for future research or practice that you describe in depth in the "Discussion" chapter (i.e., Chapter 5).

Definition of Terms

Many dissertations include a section to define terms in the study. This section is important when you are using terms that your reader may not be familiar with or when you are using terms that have many or evolving definitions.

As I mention in "Writing Your Literature Review," you should write with the assumption that your reader is not an expert on this topic (even if all your committee members are). That doesn't mean you need to define every single term, just the ones that might be considered jargon or are not well known.

I also recommend including any definitions that have many or evolving definitions. For example, my doctoral degree is in leadership studies, and there are hundreds of definitions of leadership, some which overlap and some of which are unique. If someone is writing about leadership, they should share the definition of leadership they are using for that project. The definition could be the writer's own, or it could be pulled from a source (with proper citations). Other topics with many definitions include justice, art, and education.

In some fields, definitions evolve or completely change. For example, definitions related to social identities are constantly evolving, as we learn more about how people are socialized and as populations and communities continue to define and describe themselves. If social identities are central to your research, you may want to include what definitions you are using at the time of the writing of your dissertation. You can also mention that definitions evolve, so these definitions, which apply to your current work, may or may not remain constant in the future.

Not all social identities need defining, even if the accepted term has changed over time. For example, it wouldn't be necessary to define terms related to race, unless the evolution of the language related to race is relevant to your writing. You could define words that have changed or with which every reader might not be familiar. For example, the word *queer* has evolved from a negative connotation to a reclaimed identity to an often-used descriptor for communities and spaces.

Limitations, Delimitations, and Assumptions

Every dissertation has a section on limitations, and some also include delimitations and assumptions. Sometimes these are separate sections, and sometimes they are grouped together.

In the introduction, include these sections so that your reader knows the scope of your study. You will include in-depth descriptions of each in your methodology chapter (see "Writing Your Methodology"). For now, simply list the obvious limitations and delimitations for your study.

Include limitations that your methodology textbook lists for your research design and approach. For example, if you were doing a correlational study, you could explain how any statistically significant correlation found would indicate a relationship but does not imply causation. Consider any limitations of your sample in representing the target population. For example, perhaps you had difficulty finding participants with your initial sampling methods and had to adjust your methods or expand your inclusion criteria.

For your delimitations, consider what boundaries you drew to ensure you could complete this study within a reasonable time frame and with your resources. Perhaps you only sampled participants from a particular geographical area due to travel concerns or access or perhaps you used a small sample size to ensure you could complete the project within the timeline. Such decisions are necessary to complete research; just let your reader know what those decisions were and why you made them.

For your assumptions, include anything you assumed must be true about your sample or data collection for you to get the results/findings you need to answer your research question(s). For example, you might include an assumption that your participants answered honestly or cared about the topic you are studying.

Summary

Lastly, end your first chapter with a summary and transition to the next chapter. I recommend summarizing each section in a sentence or two, moving from the problem to your study to the next step, which is the literature review. Generally, this section is only a couple of paragraphs. It should not introduce any new information.

6 Writing Your Literature Review

The literature review, on the surface, is where you present the literature on your topic and sometimes on related topics and theories. In a dissertation, however, it is where you prove to your reader that you have a vast and deep understanding of your topic. You are demonstrating that you have not only read ample information, you understand it so deeply you can appropriately describe it, present it, and organize it in a way that tells a story. You want other academics in this field to view you as an expert, a peer who should be welcomed into their ranks.

Your dissertation includes a much longer and more descriptive literature review than is generally presented in an academic journal article. You do not just present ideas with a string of citations after each sentence; you describe studies and theories and give evidence of your understanding and the connection to your topic.

In this chapter, I describe some common ways to (a) determine what to include in your literature review (e.g., providing a breadth of information but avoiding going down rabbit holes), (b) describe the literature, and (c) organize the literature to make an argument for your study. After this, if you are still struggling with the structure of your literature review, check out the "Planning and Organization" chapter for some strategies to organize your topics and subtopics to form a narrative.

What to Include

There is no template or standard for what can, should, or should not be included in a literature review. The bulk of the chapter is generally made up of descriptions of previous scholarly research and may also include historical context of the topic, influential laws and policies, theories that can frame your problem or approach, information about the target population, and details about a narrow field of study, practice, or time periods. What exactly to include depends on your specific project and the expectations of your advisor, committee, program, and field. In general, you should include the literature that is foundational to your field of study, topic, or theoretical framework and any other relevant information that informs the problem or your study.

Recency

Sometimes, your advisor, program, or scholars in your field will have expectations about which sources to include and exclude. For example, some programs require a certain percentage or number of sources to be from the last several years or to be from peer-reviewed academic journal articles. Look through your program's dissertation guidelines, talk to your advisor, look up dissertations your committee members have approved in the past, and review the work of major scholars in your field to see if there are any trends about what to include. If your advisor or institution does not have specific guidance, focus on identifying works that are essential for understanding your topic and provide support for your study.

Determining how much "old" and "new" work to include should depend on your project. Often, scholars try to include fairly recent work (from the last 5–10 years) to show they are up to date on the topic. If your sources are all from more than

10 years ago, you may not be representing where the field is now, and you might even be duplicating work that has already been done.

There are times when it is essential to include "old" work. For example, perhaps there is a foundational study or theory upon which many scholars have built their work. In that case, you'll want to review that work directly, as a primary source. Don't just trust other scholars' interpretations of that work (i.e., secondary sources) because their biases can affect their interpretations or they could have omitted something that could be essential to your study.

Types of Sources

Generally, the bulk of the literature review should be from peer-reviewed, academic journals. While there are exceptions to this, it's important to keep your audience in mind: other academic scholars. Peer-reviewed academic journal articles are often preferred because they are written by scholars and have been reviewed by other scholars, who usually do not know the identity of the author and have determined the information in the article is valid, reliable, relevant, and worth sharing with the field of study. Peer-reviewed, academic journals also often require a statement of any conflict of interests and disclosure of funding or support, adding transparency to the process.

Sometimes, you need general, "big picture" information, such as the demographics of your target population. For these needs, it's usually acceptable to rely on sources from federal and state governments (e.g., the U.S. Census or Illinois State Board of Education) or, if the information is more specific, from well-respected professional organizations that cater to scholars or practitioners in the field.

Some organizations, such as McKinsey, Forbes, and Deloitte, also might have some relevant information for your topic, but be sure to learn about the authors, including how they are funded, their motivations, their political leanings, and so forth, before relying heavily on the work they produce. If you're feeling unsure, you can even share those uncertainties as limitations of the work or reasons to consider the evidence with healthy skepticism.

Depending on the problem you are exploring, you may want to include some historical context. Providing this information helps the reader understand how the problem originated and has changed over time. Providing historical context often shows the breadth and depth of a problem. Including such a section would be particularly helpful if you feel that events throughout time have contributed to the problem or its complexity, so understanding its origins will shed light on the problem and possible solutions. For example, if you were exploring the push for inclusivity in U.S. higher education, you might want to include an exploration of exclusivity in the origins of U.S. higher education.

Related to the historical context, sometimes organizational, local, state, and federal laws and policies have affected the problem you are studying, positively or negatively—or sometimes they just complicate the situation. Whenever possible, look up original sources, while also leaning on interpretations if you are unfamiliar with the language (e.g., judicial decisions). In the same example of inclusivity in higher education, you might want to include a discussion of Title IX legislation (U.S. Department of Education, n.d.) or the Americans With Disabilities Act (n.d.) and the changes these policies have affected on higher education.

Lastly, sometimes there are major works that don't fit these categories, or your topic area may be so understudied that you need to consider other sources, such as pieces released through think tanks, newspaper articles, other doctoral dissertations, and so on. When deciding whether to include them, I recommend asking yourself three questions:

- Does this information add something essential to the understanding of my topic?
- Does this source offer a unique perspective or idea about my topic?
- Can I find this same information in a more "scholarly" source?

Because your reader might consider it, you need to weigh the validity and reliability of the information. Give thought to the author's background and purpose in writing/publishing the piece. Do they have a narrative they are pushing? Biases? Does their background match the topic? Then, include that information, so your reader knows that *you* know this isn't an academic journal article *and* that you believe it still adds to the understanding of your context. It's even okay to frame any uncertainty as a limitation of the piece.

Sometimes your area is so understudied that you will need to look to other fields. For example, when I searched for a scale to measure the stigma of mental illness, the only studies I could find were in a military context. The scales were a useful starting point, and I used additional literature to adapt them to a higher education context. I've also seen writers studying extreme underrepresentation in a particular context pull from studies in other areas where there is ample research on that representation. For example, there are very few women in the top ranks of the military, so a student studying high-ranking women might look at studies of women in executive-level positions in corporations, higher education, or other areas where women are still in the minority and in contexts that have been studied more often. The situations have major differences, but you're showing that you're doing a deep dive to understand the problem you are exploring, including considering similar situations outside of your context. If your study is so unique that there just isn't much literature, get creative in finding leads in other areas and demonstrating the need for research in your particular context.

Theory

Often, the theoretical framework is included in the literature review. If the theory can be used to understand the problem, it might fit best in the literature review. If it is used in designing the methodology, you might feel it best fits in the methodology chapter. If your findings/results relate to a theory, you might save it for your synthesis and discussion chapter.

How the theory is used should determine how much information you include about it. For example, if a theory can be used to understand the problem, you might provide more than just a description. Perhaps its origins and authors relate to your context and should be included. If others have applied the theory to their methodology, perhaps describe those theories and how you will apply the theory similarly—or not.

I recommend checking in with your advisor before delving deep into sources on the theory and writing this section. Some advisors have strong opinions on theory and want to have a say on which ones you'll use. Of course, you can push back if you feel strongly. If you really believe your theory is the best choice for your study, make a compelling argument—which you can then use in your theoretical framework section to convince your readers as well!

If the theory you select has a visual model, keep in mind that to use the exact model or a replica, you will need permission from the copyright holder to print that model in any published work. Most academic sources have a way to identify the copyright holder and contact them for permission. Usually, academics will give permission to use a visual component of their work if it is properly credited and cited, including copyright information.

What to Exclude

In addition to deciding what to include, you need to decide what you will exclude from your literature review. There is an infinite amount of academic material out there, as it is constantly being produced, so you have to decide how to draw boundaries and when to stop. Remember, this is an opportunity to prove you have the ability to look deeply and complexly at a very narrow piece of a problem, not to solve all the world's issues. When I come across something interesting, I like to consider if it is something that is vital to understand for this particular study or if it would be better studied on its own. If I'm really interested, I'll put it in a "for-later" folder, so I have access to it if I realize it really is important to the topic at hand or I can come back to it later for a future project.

When you are excluding or limiting literature that informs your topic but is not directly related to your focus, address that decision in your literature review. I am a fan of a version of "While Topic X is important to this problem, it is beyond the scope of this study." For example, in my study on campus mental health, I wanted to acknowledge that there are socialization aspects to developing mental illness, the stigma of mental illness, and seeking help. The way people are socialized to think about these things can vary based on culture, geography, race, ethnicity, nationality, gender, sexual orientation, or a number of other social identities. While it's important to understand how different groups of people may experience some types of mental injury (e.g., trauma and discrimination) and react to it (e.g., help-seeking behaviors or masking), delving into each of those identities and their relationship with mental health was beyond the scope of my dissertation. I gave a few examples and then explained there is ample literature on specific identities and mental health, and including all of it was beyond the scope of the current project.

I recommend excluding pop culture resources and sources with definite biases (e.g., books with an author who leans heavily on their experience and opinions), particularly when there is a lot of academic research in your area. You want your reader to believe you have a deep, academic understanding of the topic, not just that you read a few things that support what you already believe. Use those pop science and opinion-based pieces to inspire and energize you (see "Motivation") to explore "academic" perspectives of your topic

Ultimately, you and your advisor will decide what to include and exclude in your literature review. Stick to a few directly relevant themes that are manageable within your time frame.

Describing the Literature

Advisors and programs have preferences about how much information you should include in describing your sources. Some allow a simple, descriptive statement with a parenthetical citation to be sufficient. Others want a paragraph or more, giving the exact context of the piece. To decide how much you should include, review recent dissertations your advisor and program have approved.

If you do not have guidance on how much information to include, a good framework is to share as much as brings more context and a deep understanding of your topic. For research studies, think again about your skeptical reader:

- What might they question?
- If there are inferential statistics, they might want to know the sample size or information about the sample frame.
- If there are direct quotes, did the researcher use one-on-one interviews or focus groups?

- If there are Likert-style ratings, was there a survey?
- If so, what was the sample size and who were the respondents?

You should also include any relevant limitations.

If a study directly supports your study or findings/results, describe it in detail.

- What was the study about?
- Who were the participants?
- What methods were used?
- In what context did the study take place?
- What were the findings/results?
- What were the limitations?
- What are the implications of the findings/results?

Your reader (likely) hasn't read every study you mention, so tell them why the study supports your point.

Include studies that contradict each other. Conflicts within the field demonstrate the need for further study. When you include studies with conflicting findings/results, give information about the methodology. For example, if a study had a finding that was completely the opposite of another study, describe the differences in methodology: target population, sample size, research design, data collection, data analysis, and so on. In describing these differences, you demonstrate that changing aspects of a study can change the findings/results, and because scholars do not agree, more work is needed: Hence, your study is needed.

Even if your reader has read all the studies you mention, they will want to know that you have interpreted them accurately and how you see them connecting to your argument. When you write to prove you have a deep understanding of the supporting literature, the descriptions you provide make your argument for you. They demonstrate the problem of your context, the solution you are exploring, or that there is a gap in the literature that needs to be explored.

When it comes to the authors' recommendations, share these if they connect to your purpose and study. You can say things like, "Author X recommended studying Y" or "Author A recommended studying this topic with B methodology," and if you're studying Y or using B methodology, you have scholars who have already assigned your study importance.

Organizing Your Argument

Smart people are going to read your dissertation, probably some really smart people. At the very least, it will be read by your advisor and committee. With academic writing, write as if your reader is unfamiliar with your topic, as if they had never considered the problem you're presenting. They are going to have questions and will doubt every claim you make. Write with the assumption your reader knows nothing.

Sometimes explaining every little bit of your argument and context will feel as if you are condescending to your reader; however, even if they are incredibly knowledgeable, the point of a dissertation is to prove *you* are incredibly knowledgeable. You are proving that you can do doctoral-level research and thoroughly understand all the steps it takes to do such research, including a thorough understanding of the context, literature, and methods.

Often, writers in the proposal/dissertation stage skip ahead to the type of academic writing they see in peer-reviewed journals.

In that type of writing, the literature is synthesized. Sometimes one sentence with one claim will be followed by three to six citations of other research that has been done to support that claim. Literature reviews in academic journals are brief because word counts require conciseness of language and content. Your literature review for your dissertation will be a whole chapter, not just a section. Save the synthesis of the literature for your discussion chapter (and for the articles you submit for publication once this thing is all over).

There is no "right" way to organize your literature review. The ultimate goal, however, is to tell a compelling story that leads to an obvious conclusion—that your study is necessary—without saying so until the final paragraph of the literature review, as you transition to the next chapter (i.e., the methodology). While every literature narrative is unique, there are some patterns I've found helpful: (a) biggest to smallest, (b) chronological, and (c) cause and effect. It's very common to have a combination, with one pattern being the overall organizational strategy, while sections and subsections might fit another pattern.

Biggest to Smallest

I've found the biggest-to-smallest strategy the most effective for most dissertations. In this organizational model, zoom out as far as possible, while staying relevant to your topic area, and then continue to zoom in with a narrower and narrower focus. For example, I often ask clients, "What is the big problem you are trying to solve?" then "What are some statistics or other evidence that show clear evidence of that problem?" With this strategy, at the start of the literature review, you want to establish a compelling problem that is either large, urgent, or drastic. For example, I studied the stigma of mental illness on college campuses, so I started with a description of how many students experience mental illness, how mental illness affects college students, and how students with untreated mental illness affect college communities. I established that a large number of college students and their campus communities are affected, directly and indirectly, making it a compelling problem for all students, faculty, and administrators.

Once the big problem is addressed, you may want to visit one of the other strategies (chronological or cause and effect), as you narrow your topic. Throughout the literature review, you want to give context and then provide the information you really want to say but first need the reader to have the context. Again, think of your reader as either ignorant or skeptical of your whole premise.

One way to organize in this way is to start with what you already have: who/what are you studying and why? Think about which pieces relate more to the big picture and which relate more to your narrow focus. Then, think about what context someone might need to understand each piece or how it relates to the big picture, filling in the gaps.

In the example of my dissertation (Krone, 2016), I started with wanting to know more about campus climate related to individuals with mental illness. When I thought about why that was important to me to study, I thought about how students with mental illness are more or less likely to seek help depending on the campus climate. On some campuses (or in individual programs or departments), having a mental illness can be seen as a weakness, one that indicates a student is not suitable for the program. In others, mental illness is the same as a physical illness: when you're not well, you seek help from professionals. I realized the big picture issue was the prevalence of mental illness on all college campuses, and my focus was on measuring the stigma of mental illness on campuses. There are a lot of gaps in context between the big picture and the narrow focus—which became even narrower as I reviewed the literature and refined my research question. Eventually, I found the following general outline to move the reader from the big picture problem to my narrow focus:

- Most students on all campuses experience mental illness.
- Untreated mental illness has many negative effects on individuals and their communities.
- Most mental illnesses have proven effective treatments.
- Students are not accessing treatments.
- One barrier to treatment is stigma.
- Stigma exists in personal relationships and in the general campus climate.
- Individuals and structures influence campus climate.
- Student affairs professionals are one population that has ongoing relationships with students and influence campus climate.
- My focus was to assess student affairs professionals' levels of stigma and their engagement with campus structures related to mental health and mental illness.

Note: My study had a deficit lens, something many researchers in the social sciences are challenging. It's something I reflected on a lot during the process. In my thinking at the time, the only way to measure mental health from an appreciative lens was in examining mental health or help-seeking behaviors. I didn't have any clear measures of either of those things due to my delimitations (e.g., time constraints and data access), so I used measures that were doable for my study—stigma—which has a proven negative correlation with help-seeking behaviors (Czyz et al., 2013; Quinn et al., 2014).

Chronological

Sometimes, a problem needs some historical context to be understood. In these cases, I recommend a chronological organization—or at least a chronologically organized section of the historical context. I see this most commonly in two situations (a) when the problem centers on a population with a shared social identity and (b) when the problem has been significantly affected by laws and policies. In both cases, showing how things have changed over time can demonstrate how the current problem developed.

When presenting problems related to social identity, I often recommend starting with the big picture, showing disparities between groups within the context to be studied. Then, I often recommend using the chronological strategy, whether throughout the literature review or just one section. I recommend this because if we're writing for the "ignorant, skeptical reader," they may find ways to assign incorrect rationale to the cause of the problem. To combat this, providing a historical context, in chronological order, can show how, over time, events at local, state, national, and global levels have impacted this population and how these historical happenings have led to deep, complex, systemic issues.

For example, perhaps understanding current teacher shortages in the United States might necessitate the narrative of how the demographics of the teaching profession have changed over time. Understanding what caused the shifts in demographics for students, teachers, and administrators (e.g., social movements, laws, policies, trends in the field, political pressures, major world events, such as the COVID-19 pandemic) could be helpful in understanding some of the reasons why people choose or avoid a profession in K–12 education.

When a problem has been influenced by laws and policies, positively or negatively, it can be helpful to describe the origin and purpose of each law or policy, in the order they occurred. While all industries can be affected by local, state, and federal government action and politics, fields tied to state and federal funding and oversight may be directly and consistently affected by the actions of politicians at all levels. Understanding how policies have positively and negatively affected the problem and solutions demonstrates to the reader how the problem has persisted or grown or how previous solutions have not been effective.

For example, policies are continually enacted, to greater and lesser effect, that affect people with disabilities. Some replace previous policies, while others build on them. Presenting the policies that have affected awareness of the challenges this population has faced or how they are able (or not) to fully function in certain spaces can give depth to the understanding of the problem presented.

Cause and Effect

Sometimes problems can be simplified to a cause and effect. One thing directly impacts another thing. For example, crackdowns on certain types of common criminal activity (cause) lead to increased arrest and incarceration rates (effect). Of course, what led to the crackdowns and the choice of which communities to target could be a previous cause of the issue. Basically, with this organizational structure, you explain direct relationships (with evidence from the literature) about how each piece in a chain connects to the next piece.

It is important to be careful when using this structure not to equate correlation to causation. Two things may be correlated, even strongly correlated, and not cause each other. For example, ice cream consumption and water park attendance rates are likely correlated, but eating ice cream doesn't cause someone to head to the water park. Instead, there's a third element (heat) that may cause both behaviors independently. Consider what conclusions you are making when presenting evidence about relationships between topics.

Summary

The literature review is your demonstration that you have done a thorough review of the literature on your topic—and possibly tangential topics, if there is a dearth of research in your area. Give enough information that it's clear to your reader that you have read and understand previously completed work and are using it to inform your research question(s) and study. Organizing can feel overwhelming, so try a few strategies to group like material and find a narrative that leads to the need for your study.

7 Writing Your Methodology

Note: This chapter is about how to *write* about your methods, not how to choose the methods themselves. This book is a guide for the writing process, not for designing a study. Your methods should be selected based on the problem you are exploring, the literature, and your research questions. There are also numerous methodology textbooks, written by well-respected methodologists, which can guide you to the appropriate methods for the type and scope of your study and inform you of the benefits and limitations of various types of methods. Your research design and methodological approach should be developed in consultation with your advisor and, if you have access to one, a methodologist.

Many institutions have templates for the methodology chapter. If you cannot find a template, see if you can locate a few dissertations that your advisor has approved recently to see if there are patterns you can mimic. If your institution does not have a template or you cannot find previously approved dissertations, I recommend using the following sections, in this order, as detailed in *APA7* (see Chapter 3, "Journal Article Reporting Standards"; APA, 2020). You may want to put in some subheadings if there are sections that require multiple pages of description.

In general, you should describe each step you took (or will take) in your study, in the order you took those steps. Of course, you will likely make some decisions almost simultaneously, but in the writing, you want to treat them as distinct choices, where each step informs the next.

In the methodology section of a journal article, writers give a brief synopsis of what they did in the study. A dissertation is different though, as you're proving that you are capable of making the appropriate decisions for your methodological choices. Because you need to provide evidence of your decision-making, you should describe what type of study you're doing and provide rationale, with citations for evidence, as to why you are making each decision.

Lean on your methodology textbooks, as there are plenty of authors who have provided succinct descriptions of why specific types of approaches, data collection, data analysis, and so on, should be done and for which purposes. Use those texts to justify your decisions.

In this chapter of this book, I describe what is common to include for all studies, and then I describe what is included in qualitative studies and quantitative studies, separately. The chapters for the two types of studies overlap significantly, but I wanted you to be able to skip ahead to the section that applies most to you and to be able to get all the information in one place. After I describe writing about qualitative and quantitative methodologies, I then go through what is common in mixed-methods studies, though mixed-methods methodology chapters have more variance, depending on what was done in the study and in what order.

Most Types of Studies

Most methodology chapters, regardless of the research design, start with an overall description of how your problem, the literature, and your research questions led to your choice of research design. Follow this with your target population and sampling decisions.

Introduction

The first paragraph should be an introduction (with no heading, as it is implied that the first paragraphs of any chapter are the introduction to that chapter). The introduction should give a general description of the methods (e.g., "This study had a qualitative, phenomenological methodology, and semistructured interviews were used to collect data from 20 women who worked in the financial services industry.") and plainly lay out the sections that will be included. This should be a pretty dry chapter, simply listing the steps you took, with rationale for why you took them, so that someone can fully understand your study.

Research Design

The level of detail you need to provide in describing your design will vary by institution. Again, I advise looking for a template or dissertations your advisor has recently approved.

With any type of study, your methodological choices should be described as stemming directly from your desire to answer your research question(s), which should be based on lingering questions you have after a thorough review of the literature. I've seen many students decide on a methodology before reviewing the literature and crafting a research question, often because they have a philosophical preference for or comfort level with qualitative or quantitative data. It's important to move from literature to research question to research design, so that you have a strong tie to the literature (and what is already known) and so that your data will provide the information you need to answer your research question.

For quantitative studies, explain why having quantitative data on this specific topic will inform the problem you are exploring. For qualitative studies, explain why you chose a qualitative methodology and if you used any specific approaches (e.g., constructivist, phenomenological, etc.) and why. All decisions about your design should be described with reference to your research question(s).

Use your methodology textbooks to see what expert methodologists say are the best methods for your situation; paraphrase and quote them (with citations) to demonstrate that you have made very intentional choices with your methodology. You'll also want to have meaningful check-ins with your advisor, as they may have strong feelings about your research question(s) or methodology.

Target Population

Sometimes the section that describes the target population—the overall group you are targeting as participants, chosen because they are the individuals who have the data needed to answer your research questions(s)—is combined with the section about the sample (the participants). However you are structuring it, provide details about your target population, how studying this population will help you answer your research questions, and how learning more about this population will lend itself to understanding or solving the overall problem you are exploring in your study. Describe who makes up this target population and what is known about them.

Sampling

For your sample section, describe your ideal sample and plan for securing that group. Include the ideal number of participants and inclusion and exclusion criteria: Which characteristics or experiences are essential for participants to have to provide the information needed to answer your research question? Which characteristics or experiences might introduce bias or otherwise detract from the information you are looking to gather? Explain why you are making these choices; the rationale should be tied back to the literature, the research questions, and methodology texts.

Then, describe your sampling methodology (e.g., purposeful, convenience, random, etc.). Describe your sample frame (i.e., what exact "list" of people you will be drawing from). Include your plan to recruit candidates. Explain if you did generalized call outs for participants, and where, when, and how you shared that information, or if you did targeted invitations and where you got candidates' contact information. Also explain how you selected participants after you had a pool of candidates, particularly if you made your inclusion or exclusion criteria wider or stricter.

> **Note:** Planning a research project is complicated, and you'll almost certainly have to make some changes to your plan as things play out. To demonstrate your competence as a researcher and academic, all you have to do is describe what changes you made and why, with a focus on answering your research question(s). For example, perhaps you learned your criteria for selecting participants eliminated too many candidates, leaving you with a sample you felt was too small. Perhaps you then changed your inclusion/exclusion criteria to recruit additional participants. Simply describe what changes you made, how that affected the makeup of your sample, and how the change helped you better answer your research question(s).

In the methodology chapter, you can include a general description of how many participants were in the final sample and if they fit your needs. Save specific descriptions (e.g., demographic information) for the next chapter (unless your institution's template or preferences indicate to describe your sample in detail in this chapter).

Limitations, Delimitations, and Assumptions

> **Note:** Sometimes these are separate sections, and sometimes they are combined. Check your institution's template or, if in doubt, present them as separate sections. You can always combine them if needed. They're generally placed at the end of the sections where you describe your data collection and analysis procedures.

All studies have limitations. The easiest way to describe the limitations of your study is to review your methodology texts to see what limitations methodologists list for your design, sampling procedures, and data collection strategies.

You should also include any limitations that arose in your data collection or analysis. For example, perhaps your sample-size goal was not met or you had to expand your inclusion criteria. Perhaps you made an error in one of your steps because it was your first time doing this type of research. As long as the limitations are in line with the methodology or are minor mistakes that may affect but not ruin the data or the analysis, all you need to do is to honestly provide that information, so your reader has the full picture of your work and knows you understand the limitations involved.

In qualitative research (and some quantitative research), it is common to discuss positionality and to describe your assumptions and biases. Sometimes positionality is its own section (as described in the following section), and it should also be described in relation to the limitations of the study. It's impossible to separate ourselves from our beliefs and biases, so in this section, explain that your positionality likely influenced some aspects of the data collection and analysis *and* the steps you took to reduce bias (e.g., bracketing, triangulation).

Quantitative research may come with the limitations that numbers have in describing complex, human phenomena. Explain the limitations of the methodology and why you felt doing a quantitative analysis would provide important information in relation to the problem and your research question(s).

Delimitations are boundaries you drew around the scope of your work. They are intentional choices to make the study doable. Your delimitations might include your timeline, your sample size, or any other element that you had to constrain so that you could complete the study within the timeframe of completing your doctoral studies. You simply cannot include everything and do a high-quality and completable research project. Instead, describe your choices and how the delimitations restricted your study; also explain how those limitations made it possible to complete the work with the data and time available.

Assumptions are things you can't know for sure but need to hold as likely true to complete the research. For example, assumptions often include that participants care about the topic of the study and want to share their experience and knowledge—otherwise, they wouldn't be participating. In qualitative studies, the researcher might assume that even though we know social desirability bias exists, participants want to be truthful. You just need to assume these things are true because (a) finding out if they are would be a completely different study and (b) asking participants if they are lying or care would have psychological effects and introduce even more bias.

Qualitative Studies

In addition to the research methods, target population, and sampling sections, the methodology chapter for qualitative studies should generally include the following:

- data collection, instrumentation, and data storage procedures (sometimes separate sections)
- data analysis procedures
- positionality
- ethical considerations

Data Collection Procedures

In this section, first describe the type(s) of data needed to answer your research question(s). Then, give a brief, overall description of how you collected (or will collect) that data, in the order you completed the steps. For example, perhaps the best way to collect the data you need to answer your questions would be through interviews, as individuals hold the information you need. Whenever possible, make connections to methodology texts. You may have several subsections, if you are using multiple sources of data (e.g., interviews, observations, document analysis, etc.).

Describe any instruments you designed, such as a semistructured interview protocol, an observation guide, a survey, or a document-review rubric, to collect your information. Explain why this instrument was needed to fit your methodology and *exactly* how you designed it. You should include references to the literature or any other source that aided you in constructing the instrument.

> **Note:** Some institutions want the instrumentation section separate from the data collection procedures. Refer to your template or previous dissertations for guidance.

Next, include how you provided materials, such as a description of the study or consent forms. Describe what options you gave for times or places to engage (e.g., time slots for a virtual interview). Talk about how the engagement took place. Describe locations and lengths of times of interviews or observations. Explain how data was recorded.

Include how data and participant privacy was protected. Describe where data has been kept and if participants' identities are anonymous or confidential.

> **Note:** *Confidentiality* means that you, as the researcher, know who your participants are but are not sharing any identifying information about them. *Anonymity* means even you, the researcher, do not know who the participants are. This distinction is important, as they require differing responsibilities in protecting your data.

Lastly, include any additional steps you took to validate data, such as document review, triangulation strategies, bracketing, or member checking. Explain why you took such steps and how these steps helped you ensure your data would be the most useful in answering your research questions. Be sure to cite methodology texts in describing these steps.

Data Analysis

For qualitative research, you should have already determined steps to analyze your data. I recommend taking these steps from a methodology text, so you can easily justify your decisions for the steps you took. In this section, simply describe the process in which you engaged to identify patterns, themes, categories, and so on. You should not yet share those motifs, as that information will be presented in Chapter 4 of your dissertation.

This section often includes which coding strategies you used and describes the steps in that approach, before describing how you completed each step. This section is usually easiest to write if you follow an approach described in a methodology textbook, as the expert methodologist has already validated the strategy.

Positionality

While the goal should be research that is free of bias, as a researcher, you are human and inevitably have biases shaped by your experiences and education. Rather than pretending you are a robot (though we know they, too, have biases, as they are designed by human beings), describe your positionality in relation to the study. You might include your social identities, which can influence how you see the world because we are all socialized throughout our lives. You could also include assumptions you have about the topic and where those assumptions come from, such as your personal experiences or professional background. Lastly, if the topic itself is personal to you, describe why and what experiences have shaped your opinions. That way, you are admitting you have biases *and* that you were aware of them during the research process. You can also include the bracketing steps you took to reduce the ways your biases could have affected your study. This section should not be a lengthy story of your life or a place to express your opinions. Instead, it should be a brief statement that acknowledges your position in relation to the topic of the study and the participants.

Quantitative Studies

The methodology chapter for quantitative studies should generally include the following:

- measures (possibly a theoretical framework, scale, or instrument; sometimes included in the data analysis procedures; often inclusive of reliability and validity of measures)
- data collection procedures (include storage and participant protections)
- data analysis procedures (including triangulation)
- reliability and validity of measures

Measures

The title of this section often matches the type of measure you used for your study or is embedded within the data collection or data analysis sections. For example, you might introduce the theoretical framework you'll use for coding, the scale you used, or a specific instrument. Give enough detail that your reader understands where you found or how you developed the measure, what the measure does for the study, and how you implemented it.

You should also provide reliability and validity commentary about your measures. If you are using a measure developed by someone else, you can simply list the testing and results included in their descriptions of creating the measure. If you created your own measure, you will need to run statistical tests and draw conclusions about the reliability and validity of the measure you're using to provide accurate, consistent data.

Data Collection Procedures

In this section, first describe what type of data you needed to answer your research question(s). Then, give a brief, overall description of how you collected that data, in the order you completed the steps. For example, "To answer my research question, I needed to develop a quantitative measure of the stigma of mental illness. I created the Stigma of Mental Illness Scale, adapting a previous scale to my context, and then constructed an electronic survey through Qualtrics. The survey was sent to 600 individuals who fit the inclusion criteria, and I received 300 responses." You should include every step and decision you made to gather the data needed. You may have several subsections, if you used multiple sources of data (e.g., survey data, document analysis, etc.).

Next, describe how you invited participants to engage with you. Explain any emails sent or phone calls made. Include how you provided them with materials, such as a description of the study or consent forms. Describe what options you gave for times or places to engage (e.g., time slots for a virtual interview).

Talk about how the engagement took place. Describe lengths of times surveys were open and the average amount of time it took participants to complete. Describe any attempts to remind participants to engage. Include how data and participant privacy was protected. Describe where data has been kept and if participants' identities are anonymous or confidential.

Lastly, include any additional steps you took to validate data, such as document review or member checking. Explain why you took such steps and how these steps helped you ensure your data would be the most useful in answering your research questions. Be sure to reference your methodology textbooks in describing these steps.

Data Analysis Procedures

In this section, list the types of analyses you will do with your quantitative data and how those analyses will answer your research question(s). For example, describe the descriptive statistics you will include to give a picture of your overall dataset; describe inferential statistics you will include to look for relationships between variables; or describe the analyses you will do to examine if multiple independent variables have an effect on a dependent variable. This can be a simple description, relating each analysis to your methodology texts, demonstrating evidence that the test is appropriate for your research question.

Mixed-Methods Studies

Mixed-methods methodology chapters vary in structure because they should include any relevant information described in the previous qualitative and quantitative sections, but sometimes those sections will be in a different order due to the design of the study. For example, perhaps a focus group was used to provide qualitative data that was then used to create a quantitative survey. In that case, the focus group process should be fully described, followed by the qualitative data analysis and the creation of the survey, and then the process of conducting the survey and analyzing quantitative data would be presented. Whatever your structure, present the information in the order in which each step occurred. Give enough information so that your reader can understand each step and how it informed the next step.

Summary

At the end of the chapter, add a summary and transition to the next chapter. Explain how the design is a great fit for your problem and research question(s) and mention the major steps in the process. Then, briefly mention that the findings/results of these methods will be presented in the following chapter.

8 Writing Your Findings or Results Chapter

Note: In general, when writing about qualitative research, use the word *findings*, and for quantitative research, use the word *results*.

You may not be able to find a template to outline your findings or results chapter because there are so many ways to present the data, depending on your research design, methodological choices, steps in data collection and analysis, and what you learned in your data analysis. In this chapter, I offer some common strategies for organization, but I recommend considering your data and having conversations with your advisor to determine how to organize these sections, mostly so you don't write everything one way and then end up having to redo the whole chapter because they want your data presented differently.

Keep in mind that this chapter is a description of what happened in your data collection and analysis, not commentary on what you found. Save your thoughts and the findings/results and integration of the literature on the topic for Chapter 5.

Introduction

The introduction for this chapter should be a paragraph or two, one summarizing your problem and your methodological choices, which are presented in detail in the previous chapters, and a second paragraph describing what will follow and in what order. That way, if your reader is curious about a specific item, they can jump ahead to that section.

Participant Demographics and Descriptions

In the previous chapter, you described your target population and what sampling methods you used to recruit and select participants: don't repeat all of that information. Instead, describe the participants, aggregated or as individuals, depending on your study.

Participant descriptions usually start with demographic information. You'll give the total number of participants and then the number of participants in each demographic group (for the relevant information you collected). For example, you might include a table with a breakdown by gender, race, age, years of experience, and position. Include any information that you collected that could help answer your research question and assist your reader in thinking critically about your data. Also, be sure to use the language they used to describe themselves and resist changing those self-descriptors for your convenience (see the Use Inclusive Language section in the "Important and Unimportant Rules for Grammar, Syntax, and Punctuation" chapter of this book).

Often, researchers include demographic information to demonstrate that their sample is representative of their target population—or that it is not, which may be purposeful or may be a limitation of the research, something you add to your limitations discussion. Sometimes researchers include demographic information so that they can consider if there are differences between groups: All people are affected by socialization, which influences what people believe and what they have experienced. If you omit social identity data, you are suggesting either there are no differences by social group or the differences are not relevant for your study.

Some qualitative researchers include descriptions of each individual in their study, in addition to or instead of aggregate demographic data. The idea with such a presentation is to humanize the participants and to treat each participant as a unique individual who differs from the rest of the sample. With this strategy, participants are usually given unique identifiers, such as a pseudonym (chosen by the participant or the researcher) or an ordered indicator, such as Participant 1, Participant 2, and so forth.

Sometimes giving detailed individual descriptions can betray participants' privacy, so demographic data is often presented in aggregate to preserve confidentiality. To make this decision, consider your research questions, risk, and what you communicated to participants prior to their participation.

Whichever approach you use, when your reader has finished reading this section, they should have a good idea of who participated in your study. They might have questions about the representativeness of the sample, but as long as you address that in the limitations section, you're covered.

Qualitative Findings

In my experience, the findings chapter of qualitative studies are often long, as you should include ample evidence, including direct quotes from participants, of the themes you identified. Because there is so much, it's important to first decide how you will organize the chapter. The most common ways I've come across are by (a) theme, (b) research question, and (c) participant.

Theme

Many qualitative data analysis methodologies lead to themes, categories, or other indications of patterns in the data. You can then present your data by pattern, with subpatterns when appropriate.

In choosing the order in which to present these patterns, consider if they are all equivalent, if they follow a particular order (e.g., chronological), or if they tell a story (e.g., cause and effect). You can use the strategies offered in the "Planning and Organization" chapter of this book if you're feeling unsure. It's also okay if there is no obvious order, as you're just following the data and shouldn't force it to be something it's not. If that's the case, you can just list the themes and have a section for each one.

Whatever order you choose, use the introductory paragraphs to describe what you will present, in the order it will be presented. That way, you avoid surprising your reader, even if some of your findings themselves are surprising.

Research Question

If you have multiple research questions or subquestions, perhaps it makes sense to go through each research question, demonstrating how your findings do (or do not) answer each question. Many advisors and writers prefer this organization, though it's my least favorite because it often reads as dry, when many times the findings are exciting! It is easy to organize though, as you just go through, question by question, writing about the findings that directly relate to that topic.

Participant

Sometimes, writers choose to organize their findings by describing each participant and their responses separately, rather than aggregating the data. This strategy works well if telling the story of each participant will answer your research question. It can be more compelling to read, if it is well written and there aren't too many participants, where the meaning of the findings in relation to the problem gets lost.

Quantitative Results

Results chapters of quantitative studies are usually briefer than findings chapters in qualitative studies. In this chapter, you are simply walking your reader through the analyses you performed and the results you received: It's a dry chapter, but it's a quick one.

This chapter is often presented step by step, with either data related to specific research questions, topics, or types of analyses grouped together, with the statistical analyses becoming increasingly more complex (e.g., descriptive statistics, then *t*-tests, then regression analyses). When deciding how to organize this chapter, consider your research question(s) and present the results so that in the next chapter, you can interpret them to respond to your research question(s). Unlike qualitative findings chapters, you don't really need to "tell a story" in this chapter. You'll tell the story in the next chapter, interpreting and making conclusions about your results.

Remember to include the sample size (n) for all statistical analyses, especially if you have missing data for some items, and always include it in tables, either as part of the table or as a note underneath the table, even if all tables have the same n. All tables should have enough information that they could be interpreted correctly if they were lifted from the text and separated from the other tables.

With inferential statistics, you should define the threshold for statistical significance (usually 0.05 or 0.01) and include the *p* value when presenting each result. That can be as simple as including ($p = 0.06$) at the end of a sentence stating a statistical finding.

You should mention how you dealt with missing data (e.g., list wise, pair wise) for each statistical test. You may want to include why you chose that method, citing a methodology text to demonstrate the appropriateness of the choice.

Present numerical data consistently, such as including the same number of decimal places for each result. All characters that represent statistical abbreviations and symbols should be in italics. For more information on how to present statistical information, see the sections on Statistical and Mathematical Copy in *APA7* (Sections 6.40–6.48; APA, 2020).

It may be helpful to present your data in tables or figures, though your text should be fully understandable without tables or figures. These items, however, provide a simplified view, present a visual way of understanding your results, or provide detailed statistical information that demonstrates your comprehensive analysis; but they are not necessary for a general understanding of your data analysis procedures. Tables are often helpful in presenting quantitative data and results, as your reader can then visually compare results. Graphs may also be helpful, if they provide visual insight into the results. Be sure they are mentioned in the text, which helps your reader understand the context of the table/figure and allows you to place the item correctly for *APA7* style. For guidance on when to use a table and when to write out your statistical information in full sentences, see Section 6.40 in *APA7* (APA, 2020).

Mixed-Methods Data

Mixed-methods data analyses should be presented (a) in the order you performed the analyses, especially if one stage informed the next; or (b) with all quantitative data analyses together and then all qualitative analyses together. This decision will depend on the design of your study. If you have separate qualitative and quantitative data, see the previous sections to write each one. If each step informed the next, write this chapter chronologically, adding transitions between each section so that your reader knows how each step built on the previous one.

Summary

At the end of the chapter, add a brief summary and transition to the next chapter. Briefly describe your overall data analysis approach and, if it makes sense to do so, a summary of the findings/results. Resist the temptation to assign meaning to the findings/results because you'll do that in the following chapter of your dissertation, Chapter 5: Discussion.

9 Writing Your Discussion Chapter

Some universities have a basic template for Chapter 5, the discussion chapter of your dissertation, but there is often a lot of variability in what is included because each study's methodology and findings/results are different. The goal in this chapter is to highlight any findings/results you feel are particularly meaningful in relation to your research question(s) and problem and to consider what those findings/results mean within the context of the literature on this topic. You may also have some surprising or even unrelated findings/results, things you weren't looking for at all, that arose from your data analysis, and these items should also be discussed.

In this chapter of this book, I go through some sections that are commonly included, describe how to organize the chapter, and give some insights on how to integrate your findings/results with the literature. This can seem like an overwhelming chapter to write, as you're bringing together *everything* you've been doing (likely for years)—but I'm going to suggest a reframing: ***This is your chance to finally say all the things you've been wanting to say about this topic***.

You've now proven that you have a deep understanding of the literature and the topic, that you can do high-quality research that passes the approval of academics and experts in the field, and that you've learned some new insights that could help in understanding the problem, the context, or possible solutions. You now have the "right" to be an expert and to provide your thoughts.

Introduction

In your previous chapter ("Findings/Results"), you described what came out of your data analysis, so you do not need to repeat yourself in this chapter. You should provide a summary in the introduction of the chapter, with a particular emphasis on the findings/results you found the most meaningful and will be describing in depth in this chapter. Be sure to also list the other sections you will include, such as implications and recommendations.

Summary of Findings/Results

Sometimes, it is appropriate to add a section with a summary of the findings/results. This section can be helpful when your findings/results chapter is really long and packs a ton of information, especially if you have a qualitative study and your previous chapter includes a lot of quotes and other evidence of your themes. In this section, omit the ample evidence you included in the previous chapter and focus on the meaningfulness of your themes or statistical results. It can simply be a summary of the results or themes you listed in the previous chapter, with special attention to the ones you will discuss in more depth in this chapter. If your previous chapter was brief, as is common in a quantitative study, this section is likely unnecessary.

Important Findings/Results

Sometimes, you'll want to highlight some particularly strong, surprising, or meaningful findings or results. Keep in mind you've already provided detailed evidence of your findings/results in the previous chapter, so this section, if you include it at all, should focus on highlights from your data analysis. In a section like this, highlight your own findings/results so your reader is primed when you place these findings/results in the broad context of the topic or field in the following sections—integration with the literature, implications, and recommendations. Here, finally, you can add some of your thoughts, interpretations, and reactions.

Integration with the Literature

Sometimes this section is called "Interpretation of Findings/Results" or something else, but the gist is that you provide commentary on your findings/results and compare your findings/results to those of previous researchers.

For this section, go back to your literature review and see where your findings/results support other scholars' studies and conclusions and where they differ from or even contradict previous work. When you find differences, look at your methodologies and see if the differences can be attributed to methodological choices—or if your research really does counter previous findings/results. Consider why.

In addition, see where your findings/results point to aspects that were not included in the previously reviewed literature. Then, see if you can find literature related to these surprises and compare your results to this new literature. You don't need to do an entirely new literature review. You just want to be sure you are considering if perhaps you just overlooked some already completed research before you claim you have groundbreaking, never-before-discovered findings/results. In doing so, you can also demonstrate that you are a committed scholar, preparing thoroughly prior to a study and then delving back into the literature once you have your findings/results.

Sometimes, this section will include a new model that integrates your work with previous literature and your theoretical framework. You may want to create a visual representation of this model for ease of understanding. Mind mapping or software programs can be helpful in creating these figures.

Implications

If you include a section on the implications of your research, you can really "go off," sharing all your opinions about this topic, as long as you tie the implications back to your findings/results and, hopefully, also to the literature or common current practices. Consider what assumptions your findings/results challenge and the effects of a new paradigm on people or the field. Consider how specific environments, such as workplace settings, should change to solve, prevent, or provide a barrier to the examined problem. Explain what specific people, groups, or organizations should be doing differently to prevent, delay, or solve the problem you have been exploring.

Recommendations

The recommendations section often has a focus on future research, and many include recommendations for practice as well.

Recommendations for Future Research

In this section, consider all the implications of your research and what is needed to further prevent, delay, and solve the problem.

- Should your study be replicated with another sample? A larger sample? A more representative sample? A different target population? A focus on a specific demographic?
- Should this problem be explored with a different research design or methodological approach to understand other perspectives or aspects?
- Was there an inherent limitation either in your choice of methodological approach (as all studies have limitations and require delimitations) or target population? Could there be another strategy that would eliminate that limitation?
- Should one of your results/findings be explored in more depth, especially if your results/findings indicate it could be a possible solution to the problem?
- Was something confusing or unresolved in your study? Is there a way to explore that topic in future research?

Get creative. Really consider what else needs to be known, and give as many details as possible. Think of it as giving guidance for future scholars—or demonstrating that your research is needed, and someone should hire you to continue doing this work! Consider what else you'd like to study in relation to this topic and make a compelling case that such research is needed.

Recommendations for Practice

In this section, consider the implications of your research for practice:

- Who should know about your research and why?
- Who, specifically, needs to make changes or fight for changes to prevent, delay, or solve your problem?
- What, specifically, should be changed as a result of your findings/results?
- Who would benefit and in what way from such changes?

In this section, you can write as if your results/findings are valid, reliable, and indicate the need for change. You now have a deep understanding of this topic, so you can give advice to individuals, people in certain positions, or people in certain fields. Again, get creative, and really think about who could benefit from the knowledge you are sharing and what they should do differently because of it.

Conclusion

While the last sections of your previous chapters are likely dry summaries that then point to the next chapter, your last section of this chapter, generally the conclusion, is the place where you can say exactly what you want to say and what you want your reader to be left with when they've gotten this far. You can even get a little "preachy," if that's what you want to do and you're looking to gain a reputation as an advocate or activist on this topic.

Think about everything you've presented so far: the literature, your methodology, your findings/results, the implications, and so on. What seems especially important when all of that information is considered together? What are you still thinking about? Where will this study lead you or others?

Rather than trying to come up with some brilliant lasting thought before writing, I suggest just sitting down and writing everything you're still thinking about. You could use a strategy I suggested in the "Planning and Organization" chapter of this book: Set a timer (maybe 20 to 30 minutes) to just write, without stopping, even if you think you're going to delete it all. See what arises. Then, read through what you wrote and see if there are some powerful ideas in there that would work great for your conclusion. You can then revise what you wrote or actually delete everything for this section and start over with this new idea in your head.

10 References and Citations

Your reference list should accomplish the following:

1. Credit the authors whose studies, theories, and information you've presented in your dissertation.
2. Let your reader know you've got evidence for your claims and point them to that evidence. You're saying, "Go ahead. Check for yourself."
3. Let your reader explore the topic in more depth if they'd like. Just like you may have looked at reference lists to learn more about your topic, you're providing that same opportunity for your reader.
4. Ensure your advisor, committee, and readers that your project is worthy of a doctoral degree because you read a ton and have the references to prove it.

While reference lists have pretty standard *APA7* formatting, some institutions have preferences about how many and what types of references you should include. Some want the reference list to include a certain percentage of peer-reviewed academic journal articles or sources within a certain period of years (to ensure you have plenty of current references; see "Writing Your Literature Review"). If your institution does not have such requirements, your goal should be to have the most *relevant* references, whatever that means for your topic.

Track and Organize Your References

A reference check is checking to see that every citation has a matching reference listing and vice versa. When I perform a reference check for a client, I cringe when I have to send back a list of 20 or 30 citations that don't have a matching listing in the reference list—though this isn't uncommon. Doctoral candidates have been compiling sources on their topic for *years*, and some of those sources are bound to get misplaced. With only the last name of the author and year, it's nearly impossible for me, as an editor, to locate sources for a client without more information, so when that's all I have, I have to send it back for them to identify and locate. It takes so much more effort to relocate a source that you found and reviewed maybe a year or two ago than it does to keep things organized up front. There are a lot of strategies for keeping your references organized, though none are perfect.

> **Note:** Citations are the brief notes in the text that indicate where the information comes from (e.g., hooks, 1994). Your references are listed at the end of the document, and in APA style, they will all include the author/creator, date, title, and retrieval information. Only references that have been mentioned (cited) in the text should appear in the reference list. See *APA7* for specific formatting instructions for various types of citations and references.

One of the most common ways to keep things organized is to use reference software, such as Mendeley, Zotero, or EndNote. Ask your peers what they've been using and try them out, getting a feel for which one works best for you. One of the advantages of these programs is that you can save all your references in one place and sort them into folders to more easily find what you need. If, in your final draft, you realize you have a few citations without matching reference listings, you can search your software database to find that source, rather than finding it all over again through your library or a search engine.

You can also use the Manage Sources feature in Microsoft Word (under References). This tool can help you connect your citations to your reference list. I caution use of this feature, however, because (a) it can be tough to edit sources with some unique formatting when they are linked and (b) sometimes Microsoft Word misformats things. When you are working through your final draft, I recommend unlinking this feature and checking the formatting for everything independently.

Formatting Citations

Citations are used to clearly indicate where you've gotten the information you are presenting. In a dissertation, any claim you make should include a citation, as your opinion on a topic, at this moment, is irrelevant. If you want to claim something, you must find evidence for your claim.

There are two types of citations in *APA7*: (a) parenthetical and (b) narrative. For both, you'll list the first/sole author and year, and if you provide a direct quote, there should also be a page (p. X) or paragraph (para. X) number. If there is a direct quote, there is generally only one citation, with a page or paragraph number, so it is clear where the information came from.

A parenthetical citation follows a sentence, indicating the information in this sentence has been gathered from the source(s) inside the parentheses. For example:

> *Sharks are incredible animals and should be protected (Krone, 2050).*

This parenthetical citation indicates that this information came from a source written by Krone and published in 2050 and that there is a matching reference listing for this source in your reference list. The way this sentence is presented indicates it is a paraphrase of what Krone said in their piece published in 2050. (While this citation is made up, that is my genuine opinion.)

A narrative citation is used when the author's name is used in a sentence. For example:

> *Bloom and Martin (2016) said, "The Black Panther Party sustained disruption as a source of power by leveraging broad political cleavages to draw widespread black, antiwar, and international support in resistance to repression."*
>
> *(p. xiv)*

With this format, the authors' names are used in the sentence, so the year of the publication, in parentheses, comes after the names and the page (or paragraph) number is in parentheses at the end of the sentence (before the period).

You should use citations consistently and frequently, particularly when there could be confusion about where a piece of information came from. They should be used when you are paraphrasing and when including direct quotes.

Citations should, however, only be used when the sentence truly represents what is included in the document you are citing. You don't want to just tack them onto a related topic, as your reader could assume you didn't understand or closely review the document if the information doesn't match. In addition, be sure you are using the same language as in the text you are citing, even if language has evolved. For example, perhaps you are citing an older text that talks about "gay and lesbian" individuals only, but in your study, you are reviewing studies involving LGBTQAI2S+ individuals. Do not update the language for the author, though you can mention that the terms are outdated.

Do not include citations when you are describing specific things about you or your study. For example, you might be describing your positionality and want to draw a piece of writing that resonates with you. In this case, make sure you add something like,

> *Drawing on hooks's (1994) work in* Teaching to Transgress, *my teaching philosophy includes an approach based on the idea of education as a practice of freedom.*

rather than

My teaching philosophy includes an inclusive and engaging approach (hooks, 1994).

Without that context, your reader may be confused about why you are citing hooks (1994) and what part of the sentence applies to that reference. Another common error I see is when a researcher describes their methodology and then adds a citation for a methodology textbook:

I chose a narrative inquiry approach to understand the experiences of service learning for first-year college students (Creswell & Poth, 2017).

Instead, use language such as,

As Creswell and Poth (2017) recommended for XYZ context, I chose a narrative inquiry approach to understand the experiences of service learning for first-year college students.

Note: Maintain the exact spelling for all authors' names, including diacritics (i.e., accent marks), capitalization, and spacing. For example, bell hooks used all lowercase letters for her name, and van Manen (2023) has a lowercase *v* and uppercase *M* in his name. Search engines and reference database tools often include errors related to capitalization, diacritics, and spacing because they rely on Western-based naming conventions and do not account for differences due to nationality, culture, preferences, and so on.

Formatting Reference Listings

The best way to ensure an accurately alphabetized and formatted reference list is to do so manually, referring to *APA7* for each unique type of entry. The APA simplified the formatting from previous editions, so once you get the hang of the four elements required, it'll be a snap to format your listings correctly.

Some software programs can create a reference list for you, complete with attention to the formatting style you are using. These programs can be a good starting point, but the final lists are often riddled with errors. While it seems like a simple reference formula will result in a perfect reference list, these programs often make mistakes, such as identifying the wrong number for volume, issue, or page numbers or assuming something is one type of source, when it is actually another.

In its current iteration, I also discourage using Google Scholar to format your listings (though this search engine can be very useful for other aspects in academic writing). The "Cite" tool in Google Scholar often offers inaccurate or incomplete reference listings. For example, it might misidentify volume, issue, and page numbers or neglect to include a DOI link or other appropriate retrieval information.

You can also use Microsoft Word to manage your citations. While this tool can be helpful in tracking your citations and references, I recommend turning this feature "off" for your final draft and reviewing these things on your own (or having an editor review them). When there are errors, they can be hard to change when the feature is on, and editing them for accurate formatting can remove the tag from a citation, and if it's the only time that source is cited, it might get removed from the reference list.

Summary

It is essential to have complete and accurate citations and reference listings, so be sure you stay organized and keep track of where ideas and quotes come from. If you do this throughout the writing process, you'll save yourself a lot of frustration at the end, when you're trying to think deeply about your findings/results and conclusions.

11 Final Formatting

It's great if you can afford a professional academic editor to complete the final formatting of your dissertation, gifting yourself the time and energy it takes to do these final pieces. That's not always feasible, though, especially if you have financial or time constraints. In this chapter, I offer a few tips on polishing up the final details and submitting a final draft that your university will accept. I include where to find this information in the *APA7* manual, as it wouldn't be legal or possible to reprint all of the guidance that is available in the manual.

Institutional Guidelines

When doing the final formatting for your dissertation, the most important things to get your hands on are your institutional guidelines and dissertation template. Most (though not all) universities have some specific requirements tailored to the expectations of the program, department, or university. Make sure you review these first, especially if there is a template that you can copy to save time and ensure you have included everything that is required. These guidelines and templates often include the order of the front matter, how to format your title page, expectations for pagination, and so on.

Page Numbers

Before you insert page numbers, consult your institutional guidelines to see if there is guidance. If there is, follow that guidance. If not, the most common pagination expectations I see are these:

- Title page: No page number, but it does count as the first page.
- Front matter: Lowercase, Roman numeral page numbers placed in the bottom middle of the page, starting at ii (as the title page is the first page).
- Chapters, references, and appendices: Arabic numerals in the top right of the page. These should start at "1" for page 1 of Chapter 1.
- All page numbers should be in a font that matches the text.
- Page numbers should be 0.5 inches from the top/bottom margin and should be in the same font—in size and theme—as the rest of the text.

The switch between two types and placement of page numbers between the front matter and chapters and starting over at page 1 can be an annoying thing to learn at the end of the process. While some people hire academic editors (like me) to deal with such things, you can teach yourself how to do this. Check out the Help options on Microsoft Word and for videos, see YouTube. I have a few videos up there for this type of formatting, as do many others (see Krone, 2021).

Front Matter

The front matter includes everything before the start of Chapter 1. Usually, front matter includes the title page, abstract, and table of contents. When there are tables and figures in the text, there should also be a list of tables and a list of figures. Many writers choose to include acknowledgments and some also include a dedication. Some universities require a copyright page, and if not, many writers choose to include one. In the following subsections, I describe what each of these pieces usually includes and how it is formatted, though again, check your institutional guidelines for requirements for your program.

Title Page

The title page always includes the title of the dissertation, though the formatting varies by institution. Almost always, it is centered. Usually, it's a few inches below the top margin. Sometimes it's in all caps and sometimes in title case. Sometimes it's bolded, sometimes not. Sometimes the title breaks naturally across the line, while other times it is broken after a colon or is shaped as an inverted pyramid. Check to see what your institution requires, and if you're feeling unsure, check recently approved dissertations from your program.

The title page also includes the author, usually without honorifics or listing currently held degrees. Some institutions will require this name to match official university records and would reflect what will be printed on the doctoral degree itself. If that is not a requirement for you, when listing your name as the author, consider that this will be an official, publicly available record. Many authors choose to include middle initials or even middle names to distinguish themselves from people with similar names, especially considering that in APA, generally only last names and first and middle initials are used. Some writers choose to use only their first and last name (as I did because having two middle names often leads people to make assumptions about my marital status, something I find to be irrelevant to my academic work). Most authors use their full, formal first names, instead of shortened names or nicknames, but again, that is your choice as an author.

The title page often includes the name of the degree itself, usually stating something to the effect of "in partial fulfillment of the requirements for a doctorate in [your field]."

> **Note:** "Partial fulfillment of the requirements" refers to the document itself, as you have also been required to engage in coursework, perform the research, defend your research, and so on.

Lastly, the title page usually includes the names of your committee members, including their held degrees and departments. When there are committee members outside of the institution, the institution or organization would also be listed. For committee member names and degrees, be sure to use their preferred spelling (including initials) and exact degrees (PhD, EdD, PsyD, etc.). Usually, only doctorate degrees are listed. When indicating departments and institutions/organizations, use the full, formal names for these entities.

Copyright Page

While you will still be the owner of your work without the copyright page, some institutions recommend or require it, to protect your intellectual property.

Usually, the copyright is centered at the bottom of the page and is in three lines:

Copyright

YEAR

Your Name

I have seen it both single and double spaced, and sometimes the copyright symbol (©) is also included.

Dedication

Dedications are usually brief and start with "To." For example: "To my parents, who have always supported my goals and were so instrumental in the process of completing this journey" or "To the participants of this study. I have so much gratitude for the gifts of your time, energy, and experiences in support of this work. You have motivated me to keep fighting this fight. Thank you."

Acknowledgments

The acknowledgments section can be a much longer and more detailed expression of gratitude for the people who have supported you and your work. It often includes thanking the advisor, committee members, cohortmates, peers, colleagues, family members, friends, pets, anyone you want to acknowledge as you close this chapter of your life.

> **Note:** The acknowledgments can be a great section to work on when you're feeling stuck in writing your chapters. It's often easier to just write in gratitude, and expressing gratitude can be energizing and reconnect you to your doctoral journey.

Abstract

Abstracts often have a word count maximum and requirement for up to six key words. Check your institutional guidelines.

In your abstract, you should briefly state the overall problem, describe your methodology, list major findings/results, and, sometimes, include some recommendations. A reader should be able to quickly read the abstract, understand the contributions you are making through the study, and decide if they'd like to read further. Keep the wording clear and concise and highlight your methodology and conclusions, especially if they are surprising or yield major implications.

Table of Contents

Requirements for the table of contents are also often listed in the institutional guidelines. These guidelines often include the spacing (single or double or a combination) and how many levels of headings to include (usually three). You should also have a dotted runner between the left-flushed headings and the right-flushed page numbers, with "Page" flush right at the top to indicate what the numbers refer to.

The easiest way to create and update your table of contents is to use the Headings feature in Microsoft Word. If you assign Headings to the headings throughout your paper, Microsoft Word can generate a table of contents for you. Use the Help features in Microsoft Word or check out YouTube videos to learn how. I have a video on YouTube about this process, too.

List of Tables/Figures

Following the table of contents, you should have a list of tables and a separate list of figures. Some dissertations might also include a list of illustrations, formulas, or abbreviations.

These lists should have similar formatting to the table of contents, with the table/figure numbers and title flush left and the page numbers, with "Page" at the top, flush right, and a dotted runner between the two.

Abbreviations and Acronyms

If your dissertation includes many abbreviations or acronyms, you may want to add a list of abbreviations/acronyms, so your reader can easily refer to that page if they forget what something stands for or if there are a lot of acronyms with similar spellings. Most dissertations do not have enough of these items to necessitate such a page.

Tables and Figures

Many dissertations have tables and figures, as they can be used as supplemental displays of information to add depth to understanding the text. The text, however, should be fully understandable if all tables and figures were removed.

Tables and figures should be formatted in line with *APA7* (see Chapter 7, "Tables and Figures," in *APA7*; APA, 2020). I will not go over that specific formatting here, but I am going to note some things I've seen differ slightly, institution to institution.

Make sure you have numbering (e.g., Table 1, Table 2, Table 3, etc., or Table 1.1, Table 1.2, Table 2.1, etc.), a title, and a caption that includes any information essential to understanding the table, and any appropriate citations. For example, for statistical tables, you should always include the sample size used in the calculations (i.e., $n = X$) and, for inferential statistics, the statistical significance threshold (i.e., $p = .X$).

> **Note:** If you are using tables or figures you pulled from other sources, you need permission to reprint them. Usually, publishers and academic sources provide information on how to request permission on their websites. Also, usually, sources will provide approval for academic work. You'll then include that permission and copyright information in the caption of the table or figure.

Check how your institution wants tables and figures placed. For most dissertations, tables are included in the chapters themselves, but sometimes, programs prefer they all be listed in an appendix.

Tables and figures should be mentioned in the text and should be placed after the first time they are mentioned. Most programs prefer tables and figures to be placed directly following the paragraph in which they are first mentioned—as long as they fully fit on that page. If they do not fit, I've seen some programs prefer (a) they be placed after the next full paragraph or the next, as soon as they'll fit fully on one page, or (b) they be placed at the top of the next page, breaking up the following paragraph. I recommend checking on placement requirements because while you can switch things around later, it can be cumbersome to update everything once you have it set.

Tables and figures, with captions, should be placed fully on one page (rather than breaking across pages), whenever possible, and the font should not be smaller than 10 points. When tables have a lot of data, consider landscape formatting for that page or moving the table to an appendix. If neither of these options work, ensure that after the break, the column headers are repeated and that there is an indication that this table is continued from the previous one.

References

I included a separate chapter about the formatting of references, but I wanted to include some brief notes to check when doing the final formatting. In *APA7*, references are usually double spaced, with a hanging indent of 0.5 inches. Some programs, however, prefer that each listing is single spaced and that there is a double space between listings. The last thing to check is to make sure all of the text for each listing is grouped together, meaning it does not break across pages.

Appendices

Appendices are additional information that aid in understanding the study or pieces of it, but they are not essential to the understanding of the text in the chapters. Items frequently included in the appendices are Institutional Review Board (IRB) approval forms, participant recruitment letters, interview protocols, surveys used in data collection, and extensive tables. It is uncommon to provide raw data (e.g., interview transcripts or survey responses), though some advisors, programs, or institutions require these items as appendices.

References

Académie Française. (n.d.). https://www.academie-francaise.fr/

American Psychological Association (APA). (2020). *Publication manual of the American Psychological Association* (7th ed.). American Psychological Association.

American Psychological Association (APA). (2022). Singular "they." https://apastyle.apa.org/style-grammar-guidelines/grammar/singular-they

Americans With Disabilities Act. (n.d.). https://www.ada.gov/

Bhabha, H. (1994). *The location of culture*. Routledge.

Bloom, J., & Martin, W. E. (2016). *Black against empire: The history and politics of the Black Panther Party*. University of California Press.

Collins, B. (2020, March 3). *The pomodoro technique explained*. Forbes. https://www.forbes.com/sites/bryancollinseurope/2020/03/03/the-pomodoro-technique/?sh=2429673f3985

Creswell, J. W., & Poth, C. N. (2017). *Qualitative inquiry and research design: Choosing among five approaches* (4th ed.). SAGE.

Czyz, E. K., Horwitz, A. G., Eisenberg, D., Kramer, A., & King, C. A. (2013). Self-reported barriers to professional help seeking among college students at elevated risk for suicide. *Journal of American College Health*, 61(7), 398–406. https://doi.org/10.1080/07448481.2013.820731

Dreyer, B. (2019). *Dreyer's English: An utterly correct guide to clarity and style*. Random House.

Finch Care. (n.d.). https://finchcare.com/

Formanowicz, M., Witkowska, M., Hryniszak, W., Jakubik, Z., & Cisłak, A. (2023). Gender bias in special issues: Evidence from a bibliometric analysis. *Scientometrics*, 128(4), 2283–2299.

Gelb, M. J. (2000). *How to think like Leonardo DaVinci: Seven steps to genius every day*. Delacorte Press.

Greater Good in Action. (n.d.). *Three good things*. https://ggia.berkeley.edu/practice/three-good-things

Headspace. (n.d.). https://www.headspace.com/

hooks, b. (1994). *Teaching to transgress*. Routledge.

King, S. (2000). *On writing: A memoir of the craft*. Scribner.

Knobloch-Westerwick, S., Glynn, C. J., & Huge, M. (2013). The Matilda effect in science communication: An experiment on gender bias in publication quality perceptions and collaboration interest. *Science Communication*, 35(5), 603–625. https://doi.org/10.1177/1075547012472684

Krone, M. (2016). *Campus mental health practices and the stigma of mental illness: A quantitative analysis of student affairs professionals* (Publication No. 10128132) [Doctoral dissertation, University of San Diego]. PQDT Open. https://www.proquest.com/docview/1811406102?pq-origsite=gscholar&fromopenview=true&sourcetype=Dissertations%20&%20Theses

Krone, M. (2021). *APA7 in Microsoft Word: Page numbers*. https://www.youtube.com/watch?v=99iqtTOP_jk

Llorens, A., Tzovara, A., Bellier, L., Bhaya-Grossman, I., Bidet-Caulet, A., Chang, W. K., Cross, Z. R., Dominguez-Faus, R., Flinker, A., Fonken, Y., Gorenstein, M. A., Holdgraf, C. Hoy, C. W., Ivanova, M. V., Jimenez, R. T., Jun, S., Kam, J. W. Y., Kidd, C., Marcelle, E., Marciano, D., Martin, S., Myers, N. E., Ojala, K., Perry, A., Pinheiro-Chagas, P., Riès, S. K., Saez, I., Skelin, I., Slama, K., Staveland, B., Bassett, D. S., Buffalo, E. A., Fairhall, A. L., Kopell, N. J., Kray, L. J., Lin, J. J., Nobre, A. C., Riley, D., Solbakk, A-K., Wallis, J. D., Wang, X-J., Yuval-Greenberg, S., Kastner, S., Knight, R. T., & Dronkers, N. F. (2021). Gender bias in academia: A lifetime problem that needs solutions. *Neuron*, 109(13), 2047–2074. https://www.cell.com/neuron/fulltext/S0896-6273(21)00417-7

Long Walks. (n.d.). https://longwalks.com/

McAdoo, T. (2025, September 15). *How to cite ChatGPT*. APA Style Blog. https://apastyle.apa.org/blog/how-to-cite-chatgpt

Meir, N. (2020). Why we will lowercase white. *The Definitive Source*. https://blog.ap.org/announcements/why-we-will-lowercase-white

Merriam-Webster. (n.d.a). *Can you end a sentence with a preposition?* https://www.merriam-webster.com/grammar/prepositions-ending-a-sentence-with

Merriam-Webster. (n.d.b). Dictionary. https://www.merriam-webster.com/
Merriam-Webster. (2023a). Grammar. https://www.merriam-webster.com/dictionary/grammar
Merriam-Webster. (2023b). Syntax. https://www.merriam-webster.com/dictionary/syntax
Merriam-Webster. (2023c). Punctuation. https://www.merriam-webster.com/dictionary/punctuation
Omori, M. (2017). Spatial dimensions of racial inequality: Neighborhood racial characteristics and drug sentencing. *Race and Justice*, 7(1), 35–58. https://doi.org/10.1177/2153368716648461
The Pomodoro Technique. (n.d.). https://www.pomodorotechnique.com/
Quinn, D. M., Williams, M. K., Quintana, F., Gaskins, J. L., Overstreet, N. M., Pishori, A., & Chaudoir, S. R. (2014). Examining effects of anticipated stigma, centrality, salience, internalization, and outness on psychological distress for people with concealable stigmatized identities. *PLOS One*, 9(5), 1–16. https://doi.org/10.1371/journal.pone.0096977
Sharpe, D. (2024). Editor bias and transparency in psychology's open science era. *American Psychologist*, 79(7), 883–892. https://doi.org/10.1037/amp0001224
Teich, E. G., Kim, J. Z., Lynn, C. W., Simon, S. C., Klishin, A. A., Szymula, K. P., Srivastava, P., Bassett, L. C., Zurn, P., Dworkin, J. D., & Bassett, D. S. (2022). Citation inequity and gendered citation practices in contemporary physics. *Nature Physics*, 18, 1161–1170. https://www.nature.com/articles/s41567-022-01770-1
Thelin, J. R., & Gasman, M. (2016). Historical overview of American higher education. In J. H. Schuh, S. R. Jones, & V. Torrest (Eds.) *Student services: A handbook for the profession* (6th ed., pp. 3–19). Jossey Bass.
U.S. Department of Education. (n.d.). Title IX and Sex Discrimination. https://www.ed.gov/laws-and-policy/civil-rights-laws/title-ix-and-sex-discrimination
van Manen, M. (2023). *Phenomenology of practice: Meaning-giving methods in phenomenological research and writing*. Routledge.

www.ingramcontent.com/pod-product-compliance
Ingram Content Group UK Ltd.
Pitfield, Milton Keynes, MK11 3LW, UK
UKHW050333050926
475161UK00001B/12

9 798216 390312